A Year in the
Country

A Year in the
Country

FRONT COVER
TULIPS, INGE JOHNSSON
TITLE PAGE
BOWMAN LAKE AT GLACIER NATIONAL PARK,
CHUCK HANEY PHOTOGRAPHY
INTRODUCTION
PHOTOGRAPHY BY DEB SNELSON/GETTY IMAGES

© 2021 RDA ENTHUSIAST BRANDS, LLC.
1610 N. 2ND ST., SUITE 102
MILWAUKEE, WI 53212-3906

INTERNATIONAL STANDARD BOOK NUMBER
978-1-62145-719-0 (DATED)
978-1-62145-720-6 (UNDATED)
INTERNATIONAL STANDARD SERIAL NUMBER
2576-3679
COMPONENT NUMBER
116800100H (DATED)
116800102H (UNDATED)

Table of Contents

SPRING

SUMMER

AUTUMN

WINTER

WELCOME...

We think you'll agree—there's no life quite like country life. The simplicity of living "off the beaten path" serves as the perfect canvas on which to create treasured memories, and views of the great outdoors soothe the soul.

Whether your home sits at the end of a dirt road or you dream of finding peace away from the highways, *A Year in the Country* is for anyone in love with life lived off the land. Featuring uplifting stories and photos from the readers of *Country, Farm & Ranch Living, Country Woman* and *Birds & Blooms* magazines, this book offers celebrations of family traditions and tales of community unity, as well as snapshots of day-to-day farm life, glorious national parks, and wildlife found throughout the country—and so much more.

You'll glimpse summer, winter, spring and fall as you page through this book, which is divided by season. Regardless of whether you call the city or the farm home, you'll get a taste of country living with hearty recipes and smile-inspiring crafts to bring joy throughout the year.

We're grateful you've chosen to sit a spell with us and appreciate all that a life lived in harmony with nature has to offer.

THE EDITORS

Spring brings vibrant blooms of lupine and balsamroot at Oregon's Rowena Crest, overlooking the Columbia River.

PHOTO BY GARY GROSSMAN PHOTOGRAPHY

Spring

The Good Life

THE GREATEST HARVEST

Our 4-acre farm in southwestern Utah was the ideal place
to nurture an important crop—our children.

JAROLYN BALLARD STOUT HURRICANE, UTAH

Watching my children grow up in the same community where I was raised has been a blessing.

Here, on our 4-acre farm in Hurricane, Utah, the kids learned to work hard by hauling hay, building fences, caring for animals, and growing and canning fruits and veggies. And they became lifelong best friends in the process.

When my husband, Collin, and I bought our land in 1990, we said we weren't raising hay, fruit or cattle; we were raising kids. Collin and I turned an alfalfa field into a house with a barn, a fruit orchard, gardens and pastures where our eight kids (Justin, Shantel, Trinity, Chelsea, Jacob, Summer, Lucas and Heather) could roam. We also welcomed a variety of cows, pigs horses, chickens, dogs and cats. Much of what we made was inspired by my grandparents' farm, which I visited often as a kid.

Growing up, my children were in paradise. After doing chores, they could float in a half barrel when we irrigated the field, roast a hot dog in the fire ring or shoot hoops out by the shed. Our big tree-lined lawn was their playground.

When they wanted quiet time, they could relax on a "mattress swing" we made by hanging old-time springs in a tree and topping them with a mattress. In summer, if a kid or two went missing, Collin and I knew they were most likely asleep on the swing. And there were plenty of good things to eat as we picked from the orchard and garden. There's nothing as sweet as fresh peach juice dribbling down one's chin as another box is filled with this golden fruit.

Of course, the children weren't the only ones who thrived in this place. I love our 40-tree orchard as it blossoms in the spring, as it bears fruit in the summer (starting with cherries and plums, then apricots and peaches, and finally apples and pears), and as it gives way to autumn colors and rests bare for the winter.

All kinds of birds come to visit the orchard and the almost 100 trees on our land. Our vegetable garden provides as much beauty as it does healthy, fresh produce, and flowers and greenery hug our old house.

Some of the most beautiful land in all of Utah surrounds our little farm. Pine Valley Mountain is the first thing I see each morning, towering over the valley and nearby towns. In winter it is covered in snow, and in summer the morning sunlight spotlights its tree-covered granite slopes and red-rock foothills.

We live only 30 minutes from Zion National Park, where we love hiking year-round. Bryce Canyon National Park and Grand Canyon's North Rim are about a two-hour drive away. We like to visit both (and recognize we should go to way more often!).

Our cabin on lower Kolob Mountain is where we cool off in summers or tube on snow days in winter. It is nestled in the

With Pine Valley Mountain as a backdrop (top left) the Stouts (top) learned the value of hard work while doing chores such as tending the vegetable garden (middle). Above: Flowers and lush greenery surround the family home.

north boundaries of Zion. Sandstone cliffs rise behind the old-fashioned structure, and views on the drive in always leave me awestruck. The family ranch near the Arizona border has equally amazing vistas. This working ranch might find us herding cattle on the sagebrush-covered range, fixing fences across a secluded valley, or hiking up Water Canyon, where springs and wild grapes drip down from the cliff side.

I have lived in Hurricane since I was 6 years old and have watched it grow. When we built our home, the population was about 3,000, and our home was located "in the fields." The town was a farming community, but it has sprouted thanks to tourism. Today, farming is a side job for many people and there are right around 18,000 folks living here. Yet, even with the population rise, that lovely small-town feel remains. Community events such as the annual Peach Days, the Fourth of July celebration or the Christmas Festival of Trees instill a feeling of hometown spirit in residents and visitors alike.

If you are a first-timer in town, you can visit the Hurricane Pioneer Museum, hike the Hurricane Canal Trail, cliff jump into Sand Hollow Reservoir or float down the Virgin River. You're close enough to go exploring at a national park, rappel Snow Canyon's red rocks or catch a few trout in Kolob Reservoir. There are so many things to do, you could spend a lifetime here and never do it all. Sometimes our

Heather, Lucas and Jacob (holding baby Laynee) saddle up for horseback riding.

> **Some of the most beautiful land in Utah surrounds our little farm."**

recreation is just enjoying the work there is to do! You are always welcome to help us haul hay or cut a load of wood.

Even though Hurricane has seen huge growth, we are lucky to be in an oasis of "country" with acres and acres of fields around us. Our little piece of heaven with a panoramic view has remained much the same for almost 30 years.

Our children are grown up now, either off to college, or married with college degrees and jobs. Some have begun to move back to Hurricane to settle as they start their own families. The greatest gift we're received from our little farm is the eight kids now planting crops of their own.

When they come home to visit, I hear the basketball bouncing after eggs are gathered or the mattress swing creaking as its rhythm lulls my grandkids to sleep. Oh, yes, this little farm will produce good crops for many years to come.

The family cabin on lower Kolob Mountain in Zion National Park was built in 1957; Mylah and Marek sail irrigation waters.

MY KENTUCKY HOME

The days are long and the work is hard, but there's nowhere else
I'd rather be than on the land my family farmed for generations.

WHITNEY SHIRLEY BROWN KNOB LICK, KENTUCKY

To most people, Knob Lick, Kentucky, is a small community with a funny name, winding back roads and lots of grazing cows. The population is 486. The nearest mall is about an hour away, and you will probably get stuck behind a tractor on your way.

Named in 1867 for a stream of water (a lick) located south of a hill (a knob) in south-central Kentucky, Knob Lick has been my home for 32 years. The daughter of an eighth-generation farmer, I'm proud to carry on this tradition of cultivating and tending the land.

When I sit on my front porch absorbing the view, I see beyond the breathtaking sunset or the pristine white clouds in a blue sky. To me, the view means much more. It symbolizes generations of sweat and prayers that have been put into the land I will someday call mine. The view reminds me of hours I worked alongside my grandfather, listening to his stories, watching him work on the tractors and "helping" build something he likely didn't need my help building. Here, Dad grew up picking blackberries, shooting basketball on the side of an old barn and running around barefoot with his favorite collie dog, Tippy.

As for me, I had a childhood much like Dad's. I've been chased by chickens, dragged newborn calves out of the mud, eaten cherry tomatoes off the vine and napped under many shade trees on this beautiful land.

Nana, my grandmother, is 89 years old and now moves a little slower than the woman who just a few years ago tended a sprawling garden, sat at the picnic table shelling peas, hung Granddaddy's clothes on the line and rang the dinner bell right around noon. But she still cooks us lunch every Saturday. We come in from work at 11:30 a.m. on the dot to her homemade biscuits, extra-sweet tea and chocolate pie with meringue that melts in your mouth.

Our way of life is worth holding on to. We do that by remembering stories and passing them down from one generation to the next.

Small glimpses of the past are embedded in the scenery and the structures that surround us every day. There is a monument out back that was erected in honor of Thomas and Mollie Shirley, the first generation of our family to settle in this area in 1798. It is next to where their house stood at the time. A spring bubbles up beside the monument, and it is said that a road used to go past there and that the spring served as a place where travelers could water their horses in passing. Now, over 200 years later, we use that spring to water our cows.

I am sure I could find a town with more shopping malls, wider roads and faster traffic, but I would miss the view from my front porch. I would miss working on the same land that my great-great-great-grandfather worked up with his mules and plow. And I would miss walking through the barns that my grandfather built with his hands.

There are days when I work from sunrise to sundown. There are days during calving season when I ask myself why I chose to pursue this way of life. I have a bachelor's degree in agriculture, and I suppose I could be sitting behind a desk with no mud on my clothes, no ice to chop in the winter and no cows to feed every waking day (that includes holidays and birthdays and the weekend). Working on a family farm isn't the easiest way of life, but it's a very rewarding one.

Glancing out over a field of freshly rolled hay, watching a baby calf I nursed back to health finally take off running, and seeing the first sprouts of alfalfa I sowed peek through the ground are all just fruits of my labors. And it's a labor of love for my land, my animals, my family and my way of life.

Of course, it's not all work and no play around here. Sometimes I manage to find time to sneak off with my husband, Steve, and my stepdaughter, Savannah. We just love to explore the extraordinary natural beauty of Kentucky.

Mammoth Cave National Park, which has the longest cave system in the world,

Whitney sees fields of plenty (far left) from her Nana's porch (above). Whitney and her husband, Steve, sneak in a hike at Barren River Lake State Resort Park in Lucas (right).

is only 25 miles to the northwest. There we've hiked miles of trails leading to roaring waterfalls, vast sinkholes and smaller cave systems, and we've seen diverse wildlife such as deer, coyotes, bobcats, snakes and even the occasional black bear.

Natural Bridge at Red River Gorge in Slade is our favorite daytrip. Kentucky has the highest concentration of arches east of the Mississippi River, and that fact is quite apparent at this unique landmark where we bask in majestic views of rolling hills and dense forests extending for miles across the horizon.

Nearby at Barren River Lake State Resort Park in Lucas, there is a scenic walking trail that's a personal favorite of Lady and Blitz, our two Australian shepherds. Free time during the summer is hard to find, but we also enjoy going out on our friends' houseboat on the lake as well as camping and fishing when I can get out of the hayfields long enough to go.

Now, there very well might be a more extraordinary view somewhere else in the world, but tiny Knob Lick holds much more than picturesque scenery for me.

As I walk across our land, I like to think that Thomas and Mollie would be proud to know that 222 years later, the view from their place is timeless.

Whitney, Steve and Savannah (middle) hike Kentucky's natural wonders, such as the Pinnacles at Berea and Red River Gorge (top). Lady and Blitz (above) tag along as Whitney does farm chores.

RABBITS AFOOT

Naming big bunnies creates controversy in the Mansor household, but compromise ends in warm fuzzies for all.

DANIEL MANSOR PILESGROVE, NEW JERSEY

My wife, Jill, and I live on 12 acres in southern New Jersey with cats, dogs, horses and rabbits. The rabbits were a recent addition. Jill wanted the big breed known as Angora rabbits. I wasn't excited about having two 12-pound rabbits running around, but she got her way this time.

Jill wanted two female bunnies that she would call Faith and Truth, after themes in the Bible. However, Jill returned home with two male bunnies—and she kept the names the same. I told her we could not name two males Faith and Truth, but Jill refused to change her mind.

A few months later it was time to have the rabbits fixed. Embarrassed to tell the vet staff the names of these bunnies, I quickly renamed them Freddy and Teddy. When I returned home, I told my wife of the impromptu name changes. This was followed by hours of intense discussion about rabbit names. Finally, I said, "Let's name them Faithful Freddy and Truthful Teddy." She said, "That works for me."

As we ended the conversation and glanced at the rabbits, they gave us angelic looks. I'm sure they were thinking, "Just give us some peace and quiet...and a crunchy carrot or two."

Truthful Teddy and Faithful Freddy; Daniel shows just how large Truthful Teddy has become.

AT HOME IN THE WOODS

Idaho's mountain air, lush forests and pristine waters helped my husband heal, and each season brings more beauty.

MARY BOYLE CHALLIS, IDAHO

They say a picture is worth a thousand words. So, here are a few to show you the inspiring place where I live, and why I love my life in Challis, Idaho.

My husband, David, and I moved here four years ago. He had endured a third surgery to remove a tumor from his brain. Though the operation was successful, the recovery was difficult. He needed a place to heal, and retreating into the woods seemed like a good idea.

When David completed his rehab, we moved from Plymouth, Washington, to Challis, a small town with a population of about 1,000. My mother, an artist who lived in the area decades before, joined us.

There is so much beauty all around. The Salmon-Challis National Forest and the Lost River Range surround our home. Challis is an easy gateway to some of the best outdoor recreation in Idaho, and I am very thankful to be this close to any sportsman's dream.

In the beginning, David and I did as much hiking as his health would allow. Today, he hunts for deer or elk, and fishes in lakes and streams with fresh waters so clear you can see the trout or salmon going for the bait.

Shortly after we'd settled into our new home, my son gave me a camera. I love taking pictures of wildlife. In addition to hundreds of bird species, you'll find white-tailed and mule deer, big horn sheep, elk, mountain goats and pronghorn antelope in the forests. I've occasionally seen a big buck in town. In the morning, I sip coffee on my porch, listen to the birds sing, and watch the sunrise. A deer might wander into our yard and start eating the horse's hay.

Sunrises and sunsets are just magical. They seem to be painted on the sky. When the sun's rays hit the mountains, rich hues of red, orange and brown emerge. The colors remind me of the Mojave Desert. At night, stars seem close as they light up the sky. The only sounds I hear are peaceful.

Each season has its charms. In the spring, rain showers bring many pretty wildflowers to the mountains. Fawns play with their mamas in the fields. Summers are busy because we have to stock our wood pile for winter (wood is our only source of heat). After a day of cutting, we might camp or barbecue right beside a stream or lake.

When we can, David and I get out and explore. There is so much history in these mountains. The Shoshone and Nez Perce tribes were among the first people to live in these lush forests. They recorded their time hunting and fishing in pictographs

Clockwise from far left: Idyllic valley scene; Mary's mom with great-granddaughter Alexius; Mary's paintings; David casts a line.

at the Middle Fork of the Salmon River. Later, fur traders, gold miners, ranchers and missionaries came through: Their stories live in the ghost towns, abandoned mines, log cabins and cemeteries. I wonder what stories our house might tell.

All of summer's hard work pays off in the fall and winter as I warm myself beside the fire after doing chores outside. Sometimes we take these simple things for granted—the smell of pine trees, clean air and the laughter of grandchildren.

In these mountains, I watched David heal far beyond the doctors' expectations. Every day is a gift, and we are grateful for each one we have together in this place.

In the morning, I sip coffee on my porch, listen to the birds sing, and watch the sunrise."

Magnificent sunsets mark a spectacular end to the day (above). Top: Mary's grandson, Easton, is the adorable buckaroo pondering his next adventure.

BABY MONITOR

When lambing season arrives, I can't wait to lend a helping hand.

NASTASSIA ANDERSON MOUNT VERNON, OHIO

The alarm jerks me out of a sound sleep. I sigh and roll over, not relishing the thought of leaving my warm bed. But there's also excitement. Maybe this'll be the morning when I creep into the barn and discover new babies. I crawl out of bed, the cold floor biting at my feet, and pull on my worn farm jeans.

Wandering into the living room, I see our trusty wood stove needs attention. Opening the stove door, I stir the coals, encouraging them to come to life. Now it is time to face the cold. Pulling on my coat and hat, I call for Leesi, our farm dog. She trots over, her nails clicking across the linoleum. I take a deep breath, and we charge out the door.

It rained all night, but now snow hits me full in the face. *Great*, I think, *this would be the morning a ewe would decide to usher her precious cargo into the world.* Crunching over frozen ground, I cannot help but think that I'm beating the same path my grandma did many years ago.

Nearing the barn, I hear a sound that makes my heart leap—a newborn lamb's call. I hurry the rest of the way, then flip on the barn lights and there they are: one baby standing, the other just born.

I tiptoe over to them, not wanting to disturb the ewe. She is cleaning the first lamb, bleating to it softly and scrubbing it with her tongue. I turn my attention to the second lamb. The wind is cold, and this little one needs drying immediately. I gently lift it onto dry bedding and towel it dry. After a few minutes of scrubbing, I pass the lamb over to its mom. My quick peek informs me both lambs are male.

I stand, stretching my back. Smiling down at the new family, I head toward the gate and back to the house. The air doesn't seem so cold now that there is new life in the barn. Spring is here!

Helping birth and hand-feed the lambs are some of Nastassia's favorite rites of spring.

Scrapbook

1

1. PASTURE PALS

Our goat Gus is so patient and gentle with my son Dave. We have eight goats, six Angus, three rabbits, and several chickens and pigs. Dave likes to try to ride Gus; he succeeds about a quarter of the time.

TALLIE CZAJKOWSKI CATO, NEW YORK

2. VIEW FINDER

Steptoe Butte State Park in the Palouse area near Colfax, Washington, offers visitors unparalleled vistas of the gentle undulating hills and their constantly changing colors.

BARBARA ANSORGE STORM LAKE, IOWA

1

1. BRILLIANT BLUE

When I turned to start my walk at a park, I noticed a male eastern bluebird perched a few feet away. Quickly, I got my camera ready—and I couldn't believe the bluebird didn't move.

GINNY PHILLIPS OLATHE, KANSAS

2. BONDING OVER NATURE

Our granddaughter Savannah romping through a field of wildflowers with her Great-Grandnanny Nancy demonstrates how well an affection for nature can connect generations.

JOHN HILBRICH BOZEMAN, MONTANA

3. IN THE FAMILY

I have wonderful memories of growing up on a beef and dairy farm. I'm excited to share those same experiences with my granddaughter Saige Marie.

ROBIN DE SHAW PUNTA GORDA, FLORIDA

1. AWE-INSPIRING
My heart beat fast as I watched these three kits play. I didn't see Momma, but I am sure she wasn't too far away.

DEBORAH MOE CULVER, MINNESOTA

2. SWING AWAY
This was an unplanned spring night. We all sat in the yard on a blanket, enjoying one another's company, and then decided to swing. An amazing sunset ended our perfect day.

BECKY OSBORNE LOWELL, MICHIGAN

3. TAKE THE WHEEL
Little Tucker really can't get enough of "driving" tractors. Make or model doesn't matter a bit to this farm life-loving boy.

TAMARA BONTRAGER READING, MICHIGAN

SOUNDS OF THE SEASON
This finale to the night's light show stretched across the sky and struck about 2 miles away.

AARON SHAVER STAUNTON, VIRGINIA

WARNING
RIVER HAZARD

1. EASY BUDDIES

Our neighbor's grandson Sully and our dog, Harley, took a stroll at the spillway of Hamburg State Park in Mitchell, Georgia. We were camping for the week, and Sully came to spend the day with us.

DONNIE MUENGER WADLEY, GEORGIA

2. TAKING TO THE SKIES

I spotted this western bluebird in flight near Ellensburg, Washington. I've been photographing birds for a while now, and pictures like this are why I relish it!

THOMAS TULLY SEATTLE, WASHINGTON

3. SPLISH-SPLASH

Alhough she adores staying clean, my little girl Catherine put on her bright boots and twirled in the water.

MICHELLE DARDEN JEANERETTE, LOUISIANA

1. THE PERFECT SHOT

I've been amazed by the graceful beauty of black-necked stilts for years, but until recently, I never managed a decent shot. A local birder guided me in the right direction and, after a couple of outings, I captured this image with the sunset glowing in the background.

CLAY GUTHRIE EAST PRAIRIE, MISSOURI

2. A PLAYFUL PULL

Our daughter shares her red hair color with our puppies. At times it's hard to tell where one ends and the other begins!

DEBRA SENSENIG WATSONTOWN, PENNSYLVANIA

3. WATER MUSIC

I was awestruck by the sight and sound of the stream babbling over the rocks on a mild, rainy spring day near this creek in Upper Bucks County.

CINDI SATHRA
UPPER BLACK EDDY, PENNSYLVANIA

1

1. A BITE TO EAT
My deck is my photography studio. One spring day, I set peanuts all around me and caught a photo of this blue jay.

ANTHONY QUINN SILVER SPRING, MARYLAND

2. AIR DRYER
My neighbor across the street clearly likes the color blue. When I saw her hanging up the laundry, it took me back to watching my grandmother hand-wash clothes and then hang them on a line. They always smelled so fresh and clean.

JIM LAMBERT DENVER, COLORADO

3. MINI GARDENER
My daughter is the sunshine of my life. She brightens up every day, and she radiates happiness.

ERICA ERSIK ALIQUIPPA, PENNSYLVANIA

1. STANDING STRONG

This beautiful barn on the Nebraska-Kansas border has not one nail in it. It's all pegs!

DIXIE COLQUHOUN NEWKIRK, OKLAHOMA

2. STOP THE CAR!

We rounded a curve on Trail Ridge Road in Rocky Mountain National Park and saw these beautiful locals enjoying the spring flowers as much as we were.

CATHERINE COX NORTON, KANSAS

3. BEST OF FRIENDS

You can clearly see the bond between my daughters, Ella, 4, and Lydia, 2, and their horses. They have grown up with these animals since they were babies.

GEORGIA RITSCHER ALMA, WISCONSIN

Heart & Soul

GLENDALE CHAPEL REBORN

Emancipation set the stage for a spiritual community to thrive
in a humble one-room Georgia church.

ANNIE SHIELDS ROME, GEORGIA

Adjacent to our land in Floyd County, Georgia, Pat York and I spied a run-down chapel in a pasture. The sagging wood, overgrown vegetation and crumbling foundation gave no hint of a once vibrant congregation.

Glendale Chapel Methodist Church and School was built by freed slaves who had worked on the vast plantations of Big Texas Valley, north of Rome, Georgia. After emancipation in 1863, many stayed in the vicinity and farmed their own land.

They pinned their hopes for building a strong sense of community, spiritual growth and their young children's education on one small wooden structure.

The community held services in a brush arbor until about 1875 when Simpson Fouche, a local landowner in the valley, deeded a 0.75-acre lot to the congregation for the church. The land had two creeks running through it—an idyllic setting.

Erected in 1889, the structure was built using rocks and wood from land nearby.

You can see the ax marks where downed logs were squared off to support the floor.

The Rev. Green Johnson and his wife, Rachel, both emancipated slaves, were the creative force behind the new church. Members of the Johnson family were active in the congregation and assumed stewardship roles for 87 years.

A LINK TO HISTORY

Fortunately, Annie Johnson, grandchild of Green and Rachel, wrote a history of the church, recording major events, changes made to the building, and the names of teachers and clergy who taught or preached there. This provided an eyewitness account of its past and decline.

Annie Johnson's daughters, Jennie, Alva and Annie, became our friends. Spry women in their 80s, they paint a lively picture of life at Glendale chapel when they were young.

"The chapel was a meeting place, one of the only places we could gather and socialize," the younger Annie explains. "It became the center of our community." For the Black children in rural Floyd County with few educational opportunities, the church also served as a school for students through the fifth grade.

"Back then, there were about a half-dozen families in the church, and maybe 20 schoolchildren," says Jennie. "The littlest children sat near the wood-burning stove, with the older ones in the back." Alva adds, "We had one teacher for all the grades, and wrote out our papers on the pews, because there were no tables."

They talk of happy gatherings, from box suppers to Christmas pageants to yearly shape-note singing competitions.

"Those were big events when the surrounding communities would join us and everyone would try to outdo the other singing," says Jennie. "On the fourth Sunday of July, we always had 'dinner on the ground'—fried chicken, potato salad, sweet potato pies, pound cake, chocolate cake and uncle John Selman's ice cream made in a hand-cranked bucket."

By 1966, many Glendale chapel members had moved to town in search of jobs and to be closer to family and social connections. The dwindling membership merged with the Metropolitan United Methodist Church in Rome.

Unfortunately, once the building stood empty, pews, oil lamps, a wood stove and the church bell all disappeared. Migrant workers camping out in it did not treat it with respect, perhaps burning the wood from the walls for heat.

BUILDING FROM THE GROUND UP

After learning of the intriguing history of Glendale Chapel, Pat and I bought the land with the chapel on it, determined to pay respect to those who had built it, the faithful congregation, the building itself and its past by restoring as much as possible to its original condition.

In our area, few memorials exist that celebrate the history and achievements of Black people. We wanted to do our part to help remedy that. But where to begin?

Luckily, when we embarked on the restoration, we found builder Eric Gresham and local restoration expert Gorg Hubenthal, who were willing to take on our project. Work began in the chapel in 2014. On the last day of 2015, however, the entire building collapsed while the crew was there working on it. Fortunately, no one was injured.

Annie Johnson, Alva J. Battey and Jennie Johnson and their nephew, Wesley Kinnebrew, visit the chapel before restoration begins (far left). Above: Decades of neglect left Glendale Chapel with unstable rock footings, no doors or windows, and a nearly destroyed interior.

Today Glendale Chapel (above) has an old wood stove that harks back to chilly school days (top right) and pews facing the original pulpit (bottom right).

The restoration team agreed to view this setback as an opportunity to give the old structure a proper foundation and rebuild it stronger than ever.

We salvaged much of the original wood, and the completed building is in most ways identical to the original. A difference is that we replaced the white painted lap siding that was added in the early 1900s with board-and-batten, just as the church had when it was first built.

LOOKING TO THE FUTURE

The cupola now houses a bell that is extremely similar to the one that went missing. Miraculously, the original pulpit was located and returned after being absent for more than 40 years. And there are eight new pews, accurate copies of the originals, built by a very enthusiastic shop class at Coosa High School in Rome.

The chapel has found new purpose since the restoration was completed in 2016, hosting family gatherings, religious ceremonies and visiting school groups. It has also been home base for a science camp and a garden club event. We are delighted to see this place of beautiful, extraordinary beginnings start a new life. Jennie says, "I'm so impressed with the restoration. This helps protect the legacy of the chapel's founders, who did things despite facing difficult odds."

Quite often people who have heard about the chapel and its rejuvenation show up with cameras and plenty of questions. We are more than happy to show Glendale Chapel to visitors, but the ones we like most are those who remember it from long ago and tell us stories that add a little more to our understanding of this special place's spectacular history.

THE ROADS LESS TRAVELED

Avoid the asphalt for an authentic trip in the country.

LAURIE GIFFORD ADAMS GORHAM, NEW YORK

Turn off the main highway onto a dirt road and you're in the real country. Dust kicks up behind the car, obscuring the road in the mirror. You slow down and notice the simplicity unfolding before you.

Growing up on a dairy farm in Pulteney, New York, I was proud to live on a dirt road. My friends in small towns were surrounded by tar and pavement. The ride was smoother for cars and bikes. It was also busier—and, dare I say, ordinary?

The positives of living on a dirt road far outweigh the negatives. Most avoid travel on back roads, freeing up miles for safe horseback riding or easy walking. You're more likely to have a tractor pass you, and they drive so slowly that they don't create much dust. Country roads are the perfect place to learn how to drive; Y-turns can be mastered without fear of stopping traffic.

Mostly, I appreciate the peacefulness and opportunity to experience the wildlife that finds sanctuary here. The sweet songs of the birds aren't drowned out by the whining of tires.

Dirt roads change with each season. It is an adventure trying to navigate them during a rainy spring. The mud ruts can be so deep that driving too slowly mires your vehicle, leaving you spinning tires in the middle of the road.

I often go out of my way to take country roads, even if it takes me longer. They're a breath of fresh air away from highways.

Recently, I got out of my car to stare at a dirt road. Shallow ruts from buggy wheels, faint hoofprints, and thin bike tire tracks told the story of our rural area—the Sunday morning trek to church for our Old Order Mennonite neighbors, and their children riding bikes to and from school. I imagined harnesses jangling, hooves pounding and children laughing.

In Robert Frost's poem "The Road Not Taken," there are lines many will recognize: "Two roads diverged in a yellow wood ... and I—I took the one less traveled…"

Country roads hold a charm that I can't resist, and every chance I get, I, too, choose to take the one less traveled.

Laurie spent many hours riding her horse along Sturdevant Road, an unpaved path through blissful countryside near Pulteney, New York.

Dan Dean and Laura Kelly share the good life on Windberry Farm.

SURVIVAL OF A DREAM

When tragedy strikes, a small community helps make life on the farm possible for a deserving couple.

LISA STITES DENVER, COLORADO

Windberry Farm sits on a rocky slope tucked gently into the Ozark Mountains in Winslow, Arkansas. Downhill, many of the town's 400 or so residents gather on Saturdays at the Coffee Klatch to enjoy a cup of coffee and good conversation after visiting the farmers market.

Dan Dean and his wife, Laura Kelly, purchased the land for Windberry Farm in 2009. They built several structures, including a greenhouse and a canning shed, to get them started. Since they were trained as architects, they both wanted to make sure they got their dream home right. They moved into the canning shed

for one of the coldest Arkansas winters on record while they built their house.

After saving for 15 years, it seemed as if everything had fallen into place. "It's really the fulfillment of our dreams," Dan says of the farm they built together. "I'm so happy on the farm," Laura adds.

But in February 2015, their dream was put in jeopardy.

Laura describes Dan as a deliberate, careful, thoughtful and centered person. "He's not the type to get on a roof on a cold, slippery, damp day," she explains. "He only got up there because I couldn't reach; I tried." Laura had asked Dan for help screwing in a strap for the flue on the roof of their house. "Oh, how your life changes for want of asking for a ladder."

Dan fell off the roof and injured his lower spinal cord, leaving him paralyzed from the waist down. After that, life was a whirlwind. Dan was hospitalized, and Laura was trying to take care of him as well as keep the farm going.

For Dan's rehabilitation, a friend suggested they look into Craig Hospital in Colorado. The problem: What would happen to their beloved farm while they were away? "The community stepped up and said, 'You've got to do what's best,'" Laura says. So while Dan and Laura headed to Colorado for rehab, neighbors and friends organized care hours for the farm. Dan and Laura discussed whether returning to their farm was even feasible.

"We thought we might have to sell this place and move back to the city, where there are amenities that we don't have around here. But we wanted to stay and continue to live our dream," Dan says.

While in Colorado, the couple focused on what they needed to do and learn in order to return home with Dan in a wheelchair.

"After the injury I wasn't sure how much I would still be able to contribute," Dan says. "Adaptive equipment for just getting around the farm was an issue."

But back at home, friends and neighbors were already working on making the farm more accessible. They built a brick path and a ramp to the house for a wheelchair.

Once home, Dan faced new obstacles. He couldn't do some chores he'd done before. "Coming back here, things were more or less the same—but I'm really different."

Laura says his attitude is key to taking on new challenges. "Without his habit of dismissing negative thoughts, there would be no potential. He does it really well.

"I think it's OK to take time to adjust," she adds. "It's OK and normal to be sad. If you're not sad, then there's no contrast to happy. It's good to have both."

Thankfully, life on the farm is more happy than sad. There's a new normal, but Dan and Laura's dream is still very much alive. They harvest for farmers markets, Dan takes on some architectural freelance work, and he and Laura play in monthly "squirrel jams" with neighbors.

"I can imagine it differently," says Dan, "but I wouldn't want it to be different."

Harvesting and packaging fresh produce to sell at the Winslow farmers market keeps Laura and Dan busy in the summertime.

TAMING THE BULLY

When he had trouble at school, one young rodeo fan started an anti-bullying campaign that's sweeping the country.

LAUREN DONLEY CASPER, WYOMING

His classmates call my son "Cowboy Boone." Boone gets noticed for his height—just shy of 5 feet tall at 9 years—but also for his fashion sense. Boone wears a button-down cowboy shirt, jeans and boots almost every single day. When asked why, he'll say, "It's just who I am." He's irrepressibly goofy, wickedly smart, wildly outgoing and deeply kind. At his school, in 4-H and everywhere else, he demonstrates a heart of service that's rare in a boy so young. We're very proud of him.

Marching to the beat of your own drum can invite bullying, and, sadly, Boone has experienced more than his fair share. Last year, he was bullied relentlessly by several boys, verbally and physically. Instead of allowing it to make him bitter, Boone turned this experience into something positive; he launched an anti-bullying initiative called Buck Off Bullying.

He ordered stickers with his own money and in three weeks last summer handed out or mailed almost 1,000 of them. His aim was to get as many rodeo athletes as possible at every level to wear his sticker. Boone also launched an Instagram page (@buckoffbullying) and spread the word with a radio interview. He set up stands at a local store and a rodeo competition event on Lemonade Day, a nationwide youth program for budding entrepreneurs. He raised $653—and invested every penny of it back into his campaign.

By fall, Boone had sent out stickers and wristbands to 35 states and four countries, and he's also been featured on *American Country Countdown*. Boone wants to help other kids by expanding the goals of Buck Off Bullying: providing scholarships to rodeo schools or helping to supply gear for kids in need, sponsoring youth rodeo days for kids who take an anti-bullying pledge and who volunteer in their communities,

Kindhearted "Cowboy Boone" (center) turned his bad experience into an anti-bullying campaign.

and eventually partnering with other western lifestyle programs that help bullied and at-risk youth.

Boone hopes that Buck Off Bullying will encourage people to speak up if they're being bullied or if they see it happening to someone else. He's transformed his bad experience into an empowering campaign that can help others. Cowboy Boone wears his golden heart of service like his cowboy shirts, jeans and boots—out there for the world to see.

Josh's dogs, Beetle and Bottle, tag along as he explores the outdoors.

LIFE DOWN ON THE CREEK

Cool spring breezes, going barefoot, and hot, dusty days remind me of a free and peaceful childhood.

JOSH WHEAT BUCKHEAD, GEORGIA

Some of my fondest childhood memories are from our home on the creek about a mile from the now-defunct town of Swords in Morgan County, Georgia. I lived there from ages 2 to 7. Our home was nothing more than a shack, much like a lot of the other homes in rural Georgia at that time. I never knew we were poor, and I love waxing nostalgic about 1950s country life.

We had no running water and no plumbing. The electricity powered only the ceiling lights hanging in each room. Our heat came from the fireplace, and we cooked on a wood stove. I loved the old oak trees in the backyard, the creek down the hill behind the hog pen and chicken coop, the fields, and the barn across the road.

Although I didn't realize it then, times were hard. My father and mother worked from daybreak until dark six days a week to put food on the table and clothes on our backs. It was hot in the summer and cold in the winter with no air conditioning or central heat. That's why I lived outside for the most part—it was just as comfortable as being in the house.

Daddy raised beef, hogs and chickens for meat and eggs. He processed the meat for sausages. Oh, could Mama cook good fried chicken! We drew water from a backyard well and toted it to the house for washing and cooking. Stove wood for cooking came from scraps discarded by local sawmills. You'd find sawdust piles scattered about the woods into the late '60s.

We were a happy family living a quiet farm life that I wouldn't trade for any other lifestyle. For a child with young, hardworking parents, the rural way of life was a simple one, an easygoing world of play and of my fascination with nature.

Taste of the Country

SAVOR THE FLAVORS OF THE SEASON

EASY FRESH STRAWBERRY PIE

PREP 20 min. + cooling
BAKE 15 min. + chilling
MAKES 8 servings

- 1 sheet refrigerated pie crust
- ¾ cup sugar
- 2 Tbsp. cornstarch
- 1 cup water
- 1 package (3 oz.) strawberry gelatin
- 4 cups sliced fresh strawberries
  Whipped cream, optional

1. Preheat oven to 450°. Unroll crust into a 9-in. pie plate. Trim edge. Line unpricked crust with a double thickness of heavy-duty foil or parchment. Bake 8 minutes. Remove foil; bake 5 minutes longer. Cool on a wire cooling rack.
2. In a small saucepan, combine the sugar, cornstarch and water until smooth. Bring to a boil; cook and stir until thickened, about 2 minutes. Remove from the heat; stir in gelatin until dissolved. Refrigerate until slightly cooled, 15-20 minutes.
3. Meanwhile, arrange the strawberries in the crust. Pour gelatin mixture over berries. Refrigerate until set. If desired, serve with whipped cream.

1 SLICE 264 cal., 7g fat (3g sat. fat), 5mg chol., 125mg sod., 49g carb. (32g sugars, 2g fiber), 2g pro.

REFRESHING RASPBERRY ICED TEA

TAKES 20 min. **MAKES** 16 servings

- 6 **cups water**
- 1¾ **cups sugar**
- 8 **tea bags**
- ¾ **cup frozen apple-raspberry juice concentrate**
- 8 **cups cold water**
  Ice cubes
  Fresh raspberries, optional

In a large saucepan, bring 6 cups water and sugar to a boil; remove from heat. Add tea bags; steep, covered, 3-5 minutes. Discard tea bags. Add juice concentrate; stir in cold water. Serve over ice, with raspberries if desired.

1 CUP 108 cal., 0 fat (0 sat. fat), 0 chol., 7mg sod., 28g carb. (27g sugars, 0 fiber), 0 pro.

OVERNIGHT YEAST ROLLS

PREP 20 min. + chilling **BAKE** 15 min. **MAKES** 2 dozen

- 1 **Tbsp. sugar**
- 1 **Tbsp. active dry yeast**
- 1½ **tsp. salt**
- 5½ **to 6 cups all-purpose flour**
- 1 **cup buttermilk**
- ½ **cup water**
- ½ **cup butter, cubed**
- 3 **large eggs, room temperature**
- 2 **Tbsp. butter, melted**

1. In a large bowl, mix sugar, yeast, salt and 3 cups flour. In a small saucepan, heat the buttermilk, water and cubed butter to 120°-130°. Add to dry ingredients; beat on medium speed 2 minutes. Add eggs; beat on high 2 minutes. Stir in enough remaining flour to form a soft dough (the dough will be sticky).

2. Do not knead. Place dough in a large greased bowl. Cover; refrigerate overnight.

3. Punch down dough. Turn onto a lightly floured surface; divide and shape into 24 balls. Place 2 in. apart on greased baking sheets. Cover with kitchen towels; let rise in a warm place until almost doubled, about 1½ hours.

4. Preheat oven to 400°. Bake until rolls are golden brown, 15-20 minutes. Brush with melted butter. Remove from pans to wire racks; serve warm.

1 ROLL 163 cal., 6g fat (3g sat. fat), 36mg chol., 215mg sod., 23g carb. (1g sugars, 1g fiber), 4g pro.

CHUNKY RHUBARB APPLESAUCE

PREP 10 min. **COOK** 40 min.
MAKES 16 servings

- 1 lb. rhubarb, trimmed and cut into ½-in. chunks
- 2 lbs. tart apples, peeled and cut into ½-in. chunks
- ½ to 1 cup sugar
- ¼ tsp. ground cinnamon
- ⅛ tsp. ground nutmeg

1. Place rhubarb, apples and sugar to taste in a saucepan. Cover and simmer until fruit is tender, about 40 minutes.
2. Stir in cinnamon and nutmeg. Serve warm or cold.

¼ CUP 58 cal., 0 fat (0 sat. fat), 0 chol., 1mg sod., 15g carb. (13g sugars, 1g fiber), 0 pro.

BOK CHOY SALAD

TAKES 25 min. **MAKES** 10 servings

- 1 head bok choy, finely chopped
- 2 bunches green onions, thinly sliced
- 2 pkg. (3 oz. each) ramen noodles, broken
- ¼ cup slivered almonds
- 2 Tbsp. sunflower kernels
- ¼ cup butter

DRESSING

- ⅓ to ½ cup sugar
- ½ cup canola oil
- 2 Tbsp. cider vinegar
- 1 Tbsp. soy sauce

1. In a large bowl, combine the bok choy and green onions; set aside. Save seasoning packet from ramen noodles for another use. In a large skillet, saute the noodles, almonds and sunflower kernels in butter until browned, 7 minutes. Remove from the heat; cool to room temperature. Add to bok choy mixture.
2. In a jar with a tight-fitting lid, combine the dressing ingredients; shake well. Just before serving, drizzle over salad and toss to coat.

¾ CUP 240 cal., 19g fat (5g sat. fat), 12mg chol., 386mg sod., 16g carb. (8g sugars, 2g fiber), 4g pro.

TANGY ASPARAGUS SOUP

PREP 40 min. **COOK** 15 min.
MAKES 7 servings

- ¼ cup butter, cubed
- 1 cup sliced shallots
- 2 lbs. fresh asparagus, cut into 1-in. pieces
- 2½ cups chicken broth
- ½ cup white wine or additional chicken broth
- 2 tsp. ground coriander
- ¼ tsp. pepper
- 1 cup shredded Parmesan cheese
- ¼ cup creme fraiche or sour cream
- ½ tsp. lemon juice
- ¼ tsp. grated lemon zest

1. In a large skillet over medium heat, melt butter. Add shallots; cook and stir until tender. Add asparagus; cook 1 minute longer. Stir in chicken broth, wine and coriander. Bring to a boil. Reduce heat; cover and simmer until asparagus is tender, 3-5 minutes. Do not drain. Cool slightly. Place in blender; cover and process until pureed. Stir in pepper and keep warm.

2. To make crisps, heat a lightly greased skillet over medium heat. Place about 2 Tbsp. cheese in skillet; cook until cheese is bubbly and golden brown, 1-2 minutes. Carefully flip the crisp; cook 30 seconds longer. Remove to waxed paper to cool. Repeat with remaining cheese.

3. In a small bowl, combine the creme fraiche, lemon juice and lemon zest.

4. Ladle soup into cups; dollop with creme fraiche mixture. Serve with Parmesan crisps.

1 SERVING 191 cal., 13g fat (8g sat. fat), 34mg chol., 606mg sod., 8g carb. (2g sugars, 2g fiber), 7g pro.

LEEK TART

PREP 30 min. + chilling BAKE 30 min.
MAKES 12 servings

- 2 cups all-purpose flour
- ¼ tsp. salt
- ¼ tsp. sugar
- ½ cup cold butter
- 9 to 11 Tbsp. cold water

FILLING
- 1 lb. thick-sliced bacon, diced
- 3½ lbs. leeks (white portion only), sliced
- 2 Tbsp. all-purpose flour
- 4 large eggs
- 1 cup half-and-half cream
- ½ tsp. salt
- ¼ tsp. pepper
- ⅛ tsp. ground nutmeg

1. In a bowl, combine the flour, salt and sugar; cut in butter until crumbly. Gradually add water, tossing with a fork until a ball forms. Cover and refrigerate for 30 minutes.

2. Preheat oven to 400°. In a large skillet, cook bacon over medium heat until crisp. Using a slotted spoon, remove to paper towels. Drain, reserving 2 Tbsp. drippings. Saute leeks in drippings until tender; add bacon. Stir in flour until blended; set aside.

3. On a floured surface, roll dough to ⅛-in. thickness. Transfer to an ungreased 10-in. springform pan. Spoon leek mixture into crust. Trim pastry to ¼ in. above filling; press pastry against sides of pan. Bake 10 minutes.

4. Meanwhile, in a bowl, beat the eggs, cream, salt, pepper and nutmeg. Pour over leek mixture. Bake until a knife inserted in the center comes out clean, 20-25 minutes longer. Serve warm.

1 SLICE 352 cal., 18g fat (9g sat. fat), 112mg chol., 482mg sod., 37g carb. (7g sugars, 3g fiber), 11g pro.

MAPLE-GLAZED HAM

PREP 10 min.
COOK 1¾ hours
MAKES 15 servings

- 1 spiral-sliced fully cooked bone-in ham (7 to 9 lbs.)

GLAZE

- ½ cup packed brown sugar
- ½ cup maple syrup
- 2 Tbsp. prepared mustard
- ½ tsp. ground cinnamon
- ¼ tsp. ground nutmeg

1. Preheat oven to 300°. Place ham on rack in a shallow roasting pan. Cover and bake until a thermometer reads 130°, 1½-2 hours.

2. Meanwhile, in a saucepan, combine glaze ingredients. Bring to a boil; cook and stir until glaze is slightly thickened, 2-3 minutes.

3. Remove ham from oven. Pour glaze over ham. Bake uncovered, until a thermometer reads 140°, 15-30 minutes longer.

4 OZ. 234 cal., 6g fat (2g sat. fat), 93mg chol., 1137mg sod., 15g carb. (14g sugars, 0 fiber), 31g pro.

BANANA PUDDING

PREP 35 min. + chilling
MAKES 9 servings

- ¾ cup sugar
- ¼ cup all-purpose flour
- ¼ tsp. salt
- 3 cups 2% milk
- 3 large eggs
- 1½ tsp. vanilla extract
- 8 oz. vanilla wafers (about 60 cookies), divided
- 4 large ripe bananas, cut into ¼-in. slices

1. In a large saucepan, mix the sugar, flour and salt. Whisk in milk. Cook and stir over medium heat until thickened and bubbly. Reduce the heat to low; cook and stir 2 minutes longer. Remove pan from the heat.

2. In a small bowl, whisk eggs. Whisk a small amount of hot mixture into eggs; return all to pan, whisking constantly. Bring to a gentle boil; cook and stir 2 minutes. Remove from heat. Stir in vanilla. Cool 15 minutes, stirring occasionally.

3. In an ungreased 8-in. square baking dish, layer 25 vanilla wafers, half of the banana slices and half of the pudding. Repeat the layers.

4. Press plastic wrap onto surface of pudding. Refrigerate 4 hours or overnight. Just before serving, remove wrap; crush remaining wafers and sprinkle over top.

1 SERVING 302 cal., 7g fat (2g sat. fat), 80mg chol., 206mg sod., 55g carb. (37g sugars, 2g fiber), 7g pro.

Handcrafted

CREATE A FEELING OF HOME

TEACUP BIRD FEEDER

WHAT YOU'LL NEED
Teacup with matching saucer
Industrial glue or epoxy
Ribbon
Birdseed

DIRECTIONS
1. Arrange teacup on its side, with handle facing upward, on saucer.
2. Apply glue where teacup meets saucer. Hold teacup in place while glue sets. Allow glue to dry according to instructions on the package.
3. Tie ribbon to handle to hang. Fill cup and saucer with birdseed of your choice.

BIRDSEED WREATH

WHAT YOU'LL NEED

Nonstick cooking spray

Dried fruits (cranberries, cherries, blueberries)

1 cup warm water

2 packets gelatin

5 Tbsp. light corn syrup

½ cup flour

½ cup creamy peanut butter

Fluted tube pan

Large mixing bowl

5 cups birdseed

Ribbon

DIRECTIONS

1. Spray interior of pan with nonstick spray. Arrange dried fruit in pan.

2. Place warm water in large mixing bowl. Sprinkle 2 packets of gelatin over water. Mix until gelatin dissolves.

3. Add corn syrup, flour and peanut butter; mix well. Add birdseed and stir to combine.

4. Press mixture into pan. Let sit for 24 hours.

5. Gently flip pan over to release wreath. Loop ribbon through center and knot to secure, then hang outdoors.

TEAPOT BIRDHOUSE

WHAT YOU'LL NEED

Wooden craft plaque

Stain, optional

Hanging hardware

Teapot

Industrial glue or epoxy

Paintbrush or rag

Hammer

DIRECTIONS

1. If desired, stain plaque and allow to dry completely.

2. Using hammer, attach hanging hardware to the top center of plaque back.

3. Apply glue to bottom of teapot and press into place on plaque. Allow to dry according to the glue instructions. Hang outdoors or indoors for decorative use.

Changing seasons bring a perfect day for a kayak trip at Lake Huron's Turnip Rock in Michigan.

PHOTO BY CRAIG STERKEN PHOTOGRAPHY

Summer

The Good Life

BEFORE THE SUNRISE

On the Helt farm in Wisconsin, each day brings hard work,
fun with family and lessons in kindness to all.

DANNIANN HELT WAUNAKEE, WISCONSIN

The road to our farm climbs a long hill that drops you right by our driveway. On a sunny day, the wind turbines surrounding our land turn in the distance, the cows graze on emerald green grass and you can hear laughter as my children play in the yard.

Our farm is about 20 minutes outside of Madison, Wisconsin's capital, but you wouldn't know it standing on our land. We live in the peaceful countryside, where everything is green, open and beautiful.

In the distance, I see sparrows chasing each other through patches of alfalfa. All of the tractors are tuned and fueled, and the haybines and choppers are ready to go.

I came to this farm when Dennis and I married in 2011. I was a city girl who knew nothing about cows or dairies. I fell in love with him, the land and the lifestyle. On the farm, we work hard, caring for the land and each other.

Dennis has farmed all his life with three brothers and now with a brother-in-law.

Together they keep the family's farming legacy alive, growing corn and running the dairy. The next generation, nieces and nephews, also pitch in to help. On the farm, each person has an important job.

Dennis and I have three children: Dylan, 8, loves all kinds of sports and cuddling his kittens named Max and Ruby; Dawson, 7, enjoys helping on the farm and riding his mini dirt bike; and Delaney, 3, just adores riding in the skid steer and feed truck with Dennis and has a beautiful imagination. The boys are always up for a game of catch with their dad in the empty corn rows.

My role on the farm is to nurture our children and teach them about caring for the land. To date, my best teaching tool has been raising ducklings. The children and I discuss where they came from and how they hatched. Our ducklings are named Paprika, Lavender and Cilantro, and they follow Delaney everywhere she goes.

Dylan, Dawson and Delaney take what they've learned from caring for ducklings and apply it to all of the animals on the farm, including the kittens.

I am an avid gardener, so flower beds around our house are filled with daffodils, roses, daylilies, hostas and even more. The brighter and fuller the better! My favorite thing to do is to create dainty little flower vases and put them throughout our home. Some say the flower garden is a reflection of my personality.

This year we added a vegetable garden. The children helped me sow carrot, melon and pumpkin seeds. They were excited to put the seeds into the ground, but not pull the weeds. Maybe that will come later.

" My role on the farm is to nurture our children and teach them about caring for the land."

Clockwise from left: Wind turbines on the Helt farm; Dennis and Danniann (with their kids Delaney, Dylan and Dawson) enjoy family time; kittens are part of the farm's menagerie; raising ducklings Paprika, Lavender and Cilantro teaches the Helt children to care for all creatures great and small.

The farm is our sanctuary, and we wouldn't want it any other way. We bring our extended family together as much as we can for happy life events and holidays. Big family gatherings are an extremely important part of our identity.

To farmers, good company and a feast on the table equal happiness. In the summer, we grill out and dance on our porch as the cows graze peacefully out in the pasture.

Dennis and I have taught our children to nourish the land and that it takes hard work for what we have. It is our wish that they love and be kind to others just as they love and are kind to all of the animals around them.

We hope our children will carry on our values and work hard for what they want to achieve. And, lastly, we hope to see our children's children be a part of the farm that their ancestors started.

Our farmstead exemplifies what work, farming and family are all about. And before the sun rises the next day, we get up and do it all over again.

Danniann and the kids gather in the backyard (top). Ernie joins the ducklings for a splash in the pool (left); the Helts check on the cows (right).

PORTRAIT OF A DREAMER

My father was a man of few words, but when he said something, I listened.

KIM SON WICHITA, KANSAS

Some of us have the country in our hearts, but not the good fortune to actually live there. That describes me, and for a long time, it described my dad, Don Simonson, as well. While he was never really a farmer, he had a great love and respect for the land, which became a magnetic pull on his soul. He was a country dreamer, to be sure. Eventually, after many years, a smaller version of his dream finally came true.

Dad was a handsome man with a likable face that people found easy to trust, and a heart as big as the Kansas prairie, where we lived. Popsy, as I nicknamed him, was a firstborn with two younger brothers. He was an Eagle Scout, an intelligent student and as amiable as they come. Even though Dad became a businessman, he longed for the smell of the earth and the country's wide-open spaces.

My family lived in the town portion of a farm community in central Kansas. Dad and I both loved being outdoors. And his ever-present life message was "If you're gonna do a job, do it right!" His version was more colorful.

That message is etched deeply in my consciousness, along with the sound of his voice. Popsy believed in fairness, and he taught me everybody deserves a chance. When I was young, Popsy worked as the manager of a local automotive parts store. In 1965, he began a new business venture in real estate. He was a fast learner and a good networker, and soon he had built a modest success.

Finally, in 1985, Dad got close to his dream. On a parcel of 10 acres north of town, Dad bought his own little farm. He loved that place, even though it required hours of mowing on a regular basis. He didn't grow crops, but he indulged his "farmer instincts" by planting a variety of trees and a big garden filled with tomatoes, cucumbers, peppers, corn and watermelon. My family teased him, however, about "growing cats." A stray female showed up one day, and every four months or so after that, we had a new batch of kittens. Thus, we dubbed it The Cat Farm.

His prized possession was his tractor. I never saw his face more peaceful than when he was at the steering wheel of that tractor. It was as though he belonged there and had finally come home.

Pure contentment shone on his face when he pulled a chair up at dinner, weary with the fatigue that comes from long hours of honest labor. That's what country living meant to Popsy—a labor of love and a dream come true at last.

I still carry a bit of that dream in my heart, too. We often live our lives not realizing that we have become an example to someone else, but the legacy is there. Maybe that's why I love the feel of my hair being tossed in the wind, the warm sun on my face and the fatigue in my bones after a good day's work. It's the country dreamer still living his dreams...in me.

Popsy loved driving his tractor.

Caroline (above, with little sister Vivian) helps with several chores on the farm.

ALL IN A DAY'S WORK

This teen farmer learns that no matter the season, the best view is always the one from the barn.

CAROLINE L. BULCHER BERTHA, MINNESOTA

Down a scenic road in Todd County, Minnesota, is a busy little farm with a lot of plants and animals that need nurturing. I live here on the farm with my parents, Nathan and Anna, and my brothers and sisters: Jedd, 17; Dale, 15; Pascal, 13; Stewart, 11; twins Lucy and Winston, 10; Eugene, 7; and Vivian, 1.

In the morning as the golden sun rises, the last of the deer disappear into the dark safety of the woods. When everyone has awakened and eaten breakfast, we head out to care for our variety of animals.

While the calves stand eagerly in their stalls, the cows wait at the gate to be milked. The cats sit patiently, knowing that they will soon receive their share of warm, foamy delights.

On fall and winter days, we go out to feed the beef cows their hay. We spend lots of time cooking and baking, filling the furnace with wood (cut and stacked during spring and summer), scraping snow and attending school at home.

Wintertime fun includes riding our snowmobiles in the fields, sledding down hills and other cold-weather activities.

At all times of year, Dad services and repairs John Deere equipment, and we all help him do that.

On spring and summer days, the cows simply graze. After they have been taken care of for the morning, we turn our focus to providing fresh feed and water for the poults (chickens raised for consumption). The little ducklings and goslings eat, too.

After feeding, it's time to collect eggs. When my siblings and I open the door to the chicken coop, the hens, which have already laid a fair portion of eggs, greet us with much squawking. They, too, receive fresh feed and water.

Once we complete all of our morning chores, we proceed with our very unpredictable day.

Summer is a busy season as we work together to prepare for the long, cold winter. We bale hay when we can and tackle the much-disliked job of weeding the garden. Everyone knows it must be done in order to have good, healthy fruits and vegetables. On other days, we might harvest fresh vegetables grown to plump perfection or ripe, juicy fruits.

After harvest, we're in the kitchen chopping, grinding and dicing peppers, apples, plums, corn, potatoes, and many

Anna and the boys return with a load of wood (top). Caroline cares for chicks like these sweet animals (middle); Rodeo is ready for lunch (above).

Jedd and Dale (right) move firewood while the other family members feed the cattle (above).

varieties of berries and cherries. We can or freeze the food so we will have a taste of summer in the winter.

Of course, not all chores are the same each day. Sometimes we stay up late at night caring for a sick animal, guiding it to eat and live. Or we're surprised with a new litter of kittens or a healthy, playful calf (sometimes two or three).

At the end of a long, hot day, we retreat across the road into the cool, shady woods bursting with sweet-smelling flowers. On the way we might see a bird fly from its hiding place. On other evenings we have supper on the lawn, taking in the lovely surroundings and nice weather. When it gets dark and the stars start to shine, we catch fireflies and let them go inside. It's quite a sight! When the long day is done, it is time to hit the hay.

I love this place and what we do here, growing our own food and caring for the animals and the land. There's nowhere else I'd rather live!

OLD-FASHIONED RESCUE

Sometimes the old ways succeed where modern technology fails.

KAY FLOWERS SUMMERFIELD, OHIO

Living close to a lovely Amish community, my husband and I often transport our neighbors into town for shopping. One rainy day, we offered to drive some Amish friends to several stores because they were planning a birthday party. The rain kept pouring as they shopped, and we watched with a nervous eye as the streams rose higher.

On the way home, the roads began to flood. By the time we reached the entrance to our friends' farm, water was gushing over the culvert. There was no way to get the car up to the house to unload without getting stuck. We sat for several moments, pondering our rainy predicament. Then my husband suggested we drive to our house first to get our truck, because it was higher off the ground and had a better chance of making it through the water.

Everyone agreed, but as we started to pull away, Sarah said, "Wait! Look!"

One of her sons had hitched up a buggy to their horse, Old Reliable, and was driving it down their driveway. Without any hesitation, the horse sloshed through the water swirling well above his knees, turned around on the road and obediently halted. Looking drenched and rather bored, he stood there and waited for further instruction from his driver.

We stuffed our neighbors and all of their packages into the waiting buggy, laughing and commenting on this perfect solution. As deep as the water was, even our truck would not have made it.

The modern world with its technology had no solution that would have worked better than this. Sometimes the old ways work the best!

Kay and her friends found traditional methods of travel, like the horse-drawn buggy, can solve problems better than high-tech trucks.

THE ART OF PORCH SITTING

Pull up a chair, pour some sweet tea and relax a while as readers share their favorite country pastime.

A few years ago, my husband and I moved into a renovated 1920s house in western Oklahoma. We wanted to live in a smaller home for our retirement years. The feature that really sold me on the house was its large front porch with a swing.

Early mornings beckon my husband, still in his pajamas with coffee in hand, to the porch swing. I enjoy a little porch sitting in the early evening (but not in pajamas or my nightgown because the traffic is too close).

One outcome of post-World War II American life was the decline of front porches. More ranch-style homes sprang up in the '50s and '60s. With the absence of front porches, plus the addition of fences

dividing yards, America lost a small piece of its social identity. Sadly, not knowing your neighbor, or avoiding your neighbor, became a new norm.

Long before air conditioning, radio, television and smartphones, families often congregated on their porches in the late afternoon and evening. It was a time for relaxation and light conversation, a time to forget the cares of the day and let one's mind melt into a soft sunset.

In our little rural town, I often drive by a beautiful old Victorian residence owned by Jeff and Emily. I envision a family on that porch around the turn of the 20th century. I imagine hearing the sounds of dinner dishes being stacked up on the counter and the squeaky screen door in need of repair as the family gathers on the porch, savoring cool drinks. Conversation and laughter float into the atmosphere.

Friendly neighbors, as well as strangers strolling by, say hello. Soon heaven's light slumbers, and the street lamps are lit. All is at peace. Simplicity can be so sweet.

PAULINE RINGER ELK CITY, OKLAHOMA

A WINDOW TO THE WORLD

Our front porch drew folks like moths to a flame. It seemed as though we spent every evening on the porch, viewing our little world. No TV was needed.

I recall Friday night was date night for the teenage girl across the street. Her boyfriend gallantly drove up, ran to the house and then walked with her back to the car, romantically opening her car door and driving off.

Neighbors strolled by our home after dinner, said "Hi,"and the next thing I knew my parents had invited them to sit on the glider. Sometimes they stayed for hours and other neighbors joined in.

Toward dusk, while the house cooled down inside, my mom took her bath. She then put on her gown and duster to join my father back on the porch, where we shared ice cream. I look back fondly on those memories with a smile on my face.

ELAINE WRIGHT PUEBLO WEST, DELAWARE

THE GATHERING PLACE

I've always loved front porches. To me, they represent small-town America. Porches are where neighbors gather, where you wave to passing cars, and where you snuggle in the swing, chatting while watching the kids chase lightning bugs at twilight. There's usually a hound dog lying in front of the screen door or escaping the heat under the front steps.

Daddy always called the family out to the front porch for thunderstorms, relishing the excitement of the wind and damp rainy air as the lightning pierced through dark, swirling clouds. It's a family tradition we hold dear even today.

Sitting on the porch swing, drinking a glass of Southern sweet iced tea in a Mason jar, and talking with your family and friends can't be beat. It's an essential and pivotal part of life. The best memories are made on the porch.

MANDI WOOD EASTANOLLEE, GEORGIA

This old Victorian porch has become Pauline's favorite (far left); her neighbors Jeff and Emily relax on the porch with plenty of lovely flowers (top). Mandi's porch (above) is a cozy, colorful country oasis ready-made for family and friends.

OUR POT OF GOLD

In a corner of Montana known for mining and outlaws,
my husband and I found a scenic treasure.

BETTY WESTBURG LEWISTOWN, MONTANA

Far from the hustle and bustle of crowded city streets, my husband, Albert, and I live in a place we call Whisky. Tucked into the foothills of Montana's Judith Mountains, Whisky is just over the ridge off the old Gilt Edge Stage Road, stretching way up Whisky Gulch to the west. It is a dozen or so miles from Lewistown, the geographic center of Montana.

Our roots go all the way back to the state's homesteading days. Albert and I have lived all our lives in Montana. We built our home, which sits on the lower end of the northern ridge, in 2014. We spent the past years completing the house, building some of the outbuildings, clearing brush, putting up fencing and taking care of the land. Our two sons, Dana and Nick, are grown and live in the Billings area with their families.

The views from Whisky are gorgeous. Throughout the spring and summer, wildflowers add a palette of yellow, blue, white, pink and purple hues to the green landscape. Lush meadows rise up to meet mountain foothills on the north, west and south, and to the east is an open prairie vista as far as the eye can see.

In winter, snow blankets the land, and the air is cool and crisp. Wind swirls the snow around, creating drifts that look like dollops of fresh whipped cream. When the sun shines, the snow-covered landscape sparkles like diamonds. Although it is beautiful, the snow and wind can create a challenge for getting into town and back, since we must drive up our lane and the 7 miles of county road before reaching pavement.

As we go about our daily work, we feel blessed to live in Whisky! In the meadow to the north, during the summer months, the black hides of the neighbor's cattle glisten in the sun as some graze while others lie in the cool green grass.

Some might find living way out here in the boondocks boring or lonely, but the beautiful scenery along with the domestic and wild animals and birds inhabiting the area keep us entertained.

Sam and Homer, our horse and donkey, contentedly browse in the pasture below our house near one of Homer's "wallows," a concave circle that he has pawed clear of vegetation, where he rolls in the dirt. Homer is our watchdog and will snort loudly at anything or anyone he feels is abnormal. Wild things like deer, antelope, elk, meadowlarks, hawks, blackbirds and bluebirds, bears, eagles, owls, mountain lions, turkeys, skunks, rabbits, snakes, hummingbirds, crows and moose provide no small amount of amusement.

The rich history of the area intrigues us as we imagine life as it was during the turn of the 20th century. Northeast from the ridge in the far corner of our property, Black Butte, a big lone butte at the east end of the Judith Mountains, rises above the plains. Native Americans used the topmost part of the butte as a signal point, where they built fires and made smoke signals with buffalo skins.

A few miles southwest of Black Butte, Bertie Brown's cabin stands. Originally from Missouri, she was among a small number of Black women who homesteaded alone in Montana. She was in her 20s when she settled here in 1898. Bertie was one of the best moonshine makers in the country. My grandfather traveled miles out of his way to buy her brew, which she sold by the drink or the bottle. Her place was spic and span, and folks were welcome to stop in anytime.

During the gold mining era of the 1880s and early 1900s, Gilt Edge was a thriving mining town with a population of nearly 1,500. We've heard that there were six general stores, a butcher shop, a bakery, two drugstores, a post office, a restaurant, a clothing store, two barbershops, six hotels and boardinghouses, a church, a school, a hospital, a funeral parlor, four livery barns, a dance hall, two blacksmith shops, 13 saloons, one blind pig (a liquor store that did not have a license and sold whiskey out of the back door) and a jail.

And Gilt Edge had quite a few infamous residents. Calamity Jane, a legendary frontierswoman and sharpshooter, lived in Gilt Edge for a time, and the outlaw Kid Curry occasionally visited the town.

When the mines shut down, businesses either closed or moved elsewhere, many of the townsfolk left and the town dwindled. Gilt Edge is quieter nowadays. Skeletons of some original buildings, including the jail and one of the bordellos, still stand as silent reminders of the town's past.

Mother Nature fills the silence in her own ways. One day I admire the colorful blooms, and the next I wake up to white stuff on the ground. Maybe the electricity will go out. And if it does, we'll fire up the grill to heat water collected from the snow to make coffee and hot meals. No worries, though; all is well. Here in our native Big Sky Country, we've found our pot of gold.

Scrapbook

CAPTURE THE BEAUTY AROUND YOU

1

1. AN EXCITING SIGHT

This was taken on a summer day at the Arizona-Sonora Desert Museum in Tucson. I had never seen a female varied bunting eat from a cactus fruit, so it was exciting to snap this moment.

DAWN ARJES PAW PAW, ILLINOIS

2. GRASS IS GREENER

Every time we bring the old Allis out of the shed, my kids come running! Our country life brings a joy to my kids that they never had living in the city.

KELSEY MARSH BROWNSDALE, MINNESOTA

1. SHINING BRIGHT
After a long day of hauling hay with the tractor, the stars and the lightning bugs twinkled in unison.

AMY NICHOLS ITHACA, NEBRASKA

2. LET FREEDOM RING
My great-grandsons Nathan and Isiah, along with grandson Shelby, celebrate July Fourth with juicy watermelon.

ANITA WILLIAMS DEKEN SUBIACO, ARKANSAS

3. STILL LEARNING
This cute juvenile male ruby-throated hummingbird was investigating the zinnias in my garden. I watched him as he landed on the stem of this flower and attempted a tightrope act up the stalk. All hummingbirds are fun to watch, but I think juveniles are especially intriguing with their wide-eyed curiosity.

CAROL HOLLIDAY TERRE HAUTE, INDIANA

1. PICTURE PERFECT
One day I came across this field full of daisies. Little Taylor was the perfect model to help capture summer's beauty.

KALLIE KANTOS
INTERNATIONAL FALLS, MINNESOTA

2. OUTDOOR FUN
My grandson Colton had fun with his headlight and toys outside our tent. Seeing your grandchildren fall in love with camping and the outdoors is so very precious.

MYRON CARTER
MAGGIE VALLEY, NORTH CAROLINA

3. LET'S GO FLY A KITE
Our family explored the area around our campground and found the perfect field for kite flying. Luckily, we had one!

DIANNE CRASWELL LETANG, NEW BRUNSWICK

My 3-year-old son, David, begged to visit the cows across the road from his grandparents' farm. He spent many hours of his vacation talking to his cow friends and watching the sunsets.

RENEE PRZELSKI
ADVANCE, NORTH CAROLINA

1. ALLEGHENY SUNSET

I'm blessed to live in the Shenandoah Valley of Virginia. This is the view that welcomes me home in the evenings after a long day of shoeing horses.

ZACHARY WILLIAMS MOUNT SOLON, VIRGINIA

2. SWEET TREAT

Young pups Olivia and Abby have earned a reward—ice cream—for their good behavior during a trip to the vet.

DOT BRANDENBERGER FORT WAYNE, INDIANA

3. PAPI GROWS A GARDEN

I have had the joy of watching my grandfather, Papi, and my 5-year-old son, Hunter, work together in the garden for two seasons. Who knew that a small plot of dirt could bring people together?

ALICIA RICHHART MOORESVILLE, INDIANA

1. THE CAT'S MEOW

I frequently cut a melon in half and put it out on a feeder just to see who will turn up to eat. On this particular day, it was a gray catbird.

KEITH ANDERSON PONCA CITY, OKLAHOMA

2. COOLING OFF

My granddaughter Adelyn takes a slurp from the hydrant on Mamaw's farm during the last hot days of summer.

LISA STORY WAUSA, NEBRASKA

3. PETITE PATIENCE

For a little boy's first time fishing, all that matters is digging for worms and waiting for the fish to bite.

REBECCA BALLINGER
JEFFERSON CITY, TENNESSEE

1. THE SUNFLOWER KING

Every year I plant a few sunflowers for their beauty and as a treat for the birds. One summer afternoon, an American goldfinch traveled from flower to flower, checking out the seeds. He perched on the tallest flower and looked around, almost as if surveying his kingdom.

PAMELA HOWARD PORT DEPOSIT, MARYLAND

2. STARRY NIGHT

This was the very first time I had been to Joshua Tree National Park. It was just me, the coyotes and the Milky Way on this magical night.

EMILY TYNON CALDWELL, IDAHO

3. PLAYTIME AT GRANDMA'S

There are two things that make Grandma's house special: bubble gum and bubbles. When I see the tedium starting, I ask if anyone wants to blow bubbles and all the little ones start hopping with joy.

REBECCA KOMPPA SEBEKA, MINNESOTA

1. PAPA'S APPRENTICE

My daughter, Oaklynn, is only a few years old, but checking on the cows with Dad is serious business.

TRISHA MURDOCK POCAHONTAS, ARKANSAS

2. THREE'S COMPANY

No kid can resist! Hallee, Henslee and Hunter are the three H's of our 3H Farms, and they never pass up an opportunity to play on the hay bales.

KASEY HENDRICK BOWLING GREEN, KENTUCKY

3. CABIN KIDS

We've made many memories with our extended family at our beloved cabin in Colorado, and we are now passing that joy on to the next generation.

KAYLA ANDERSON CHRISMAN, ILLINOIS

Heart & Soul

A WALL OF LOVE

Faced with health issues, I thought starting over and building new gardens from scratch would be impossible.

SUSIE GRAF POUND, WISCONSIN

The backyard is my favorite place. I spend as much time as I can in this space, from early morning through dusk. And there is a reason this little slice of heaven touches my heart in a meaningful way.

I have been a gardener, self-taught, for over 30 years. When we decided to build a new house, I did not want to leave our former home and the yard I had designed, built and maintained for 15 years. The thought of starting over was extremely depressing, especially because I struggle with crippling rheumatoid arthritis. It would be daunting to clear the land, amend the soil and dig tons of holes again.

The new property is heavily wooded with lots of shade. This was a challenge for me. Trees mean roots, big and small, tons of weeds, and underbrush. Ugh.

Our small backyard backs up to the base of a sloping hill, a perfect spot for a wall. Our last place had it all: a waterfall, a small stone wall and beautiful flower beds. I could envision all of that here.

When we first surveyed our property, as I walked the base of the hill, I stomped out the potential lay of a wall with my feet in the snow. My husband, Greg, watched me. When he realized what I was doing, he informed me he was not building another labor-intensive wall or a waterfall. He was

building a house and some log furniture. Period. Trying to convince him was to no avail. Yet I realized this landscape could be a new experience and a fun learning opportunity. My mottoes have always been "Never say never" and "Don't tell me I can't, because I'll prove I can."

Then my world was shaken to its core. I was diagnosed with breast cancer. I had one surgery and, a week later, a second. Before the second surgery, my husband dug out my sewing machine. He'd never sewn before, but he got it all figured it out and sewed seam binding to some mesh. Greg said he was making a tent. I was sleeping a lot, so I didn't ask questions.

The morning after my second surgery, Greg informed me we were going up north so he could work on the new property. I was hours out of surgery and couldn't sit on some lawn chair while he worked! He said it would be fine. When we got there, he helped me up the small hill, hastily tied a hammock between two trees and nestled me in to rest. He pulled out the mesh tent he had made and encased me within it, shielding me from the bugs so I'd safely sleep undisturbed. He could see and hear me should I need something.

At the base of the hill was a huge pile of quarry stone. Before I fell asleep, I gazed in amazement as he laid the first stones. It was the start of my longed-for wall.

Greg built it, complete with a waterfall and steps all the way to the top of the hill. It took several weeks. I call this my wall of love. I hadn't planned on landscaping any part of the hill until I saw this big piece of hardscape. It called to me with abundant love. We didn't have a budget for such a huge undertaking, so, as soon as I was up to it, I began splitting my plants at home.

The hill was landscaped well before our new home was done. After the house was built, Greg and I dug the small pond under the waterfall. We built it on our 23rd anniversary as a gift to each other. Greg was never into landscaping or flowers

before. Now we walk the property together almost every morning and Greg knows the names of the bushes and the flowers, and he tells me where he would like certain varieties planted.

In time, I also requested an arbor and later a gazebo. Greg lovingly built both. There's nothing like eating a meal sitting next to our pond as we listen to the sounds of the water racing through the rocks and splashing into the water below, or reading a book while swaying on the patio swing. I can spend hours watching the many species of birds that flit back and forth and bathe in the waterfall.

This outdoor space is truly therapy for my mind, body and soul. Our backyard is our little slice of heaven, built together with love. Lots of love.

Abundant flowers and plants flourish along the steps leading up to a gazebo atop the hill (far left). A red watering can and birdhouse add character (top); a stone pathway through the yard connects the patio to the stairs (above).

The twinkling of tiny fireflies adds a touch of magic to the horizon.

FIREFLIES AT THE BARN

A quiet evening on the farm, filled with the beauty of nature, reminds me why there's no place like the country.

MADISON FALCONNIER COLUMBIA, MISSOURI

The refreshing feel of evening replaces the warmth of day. The sound of my brothers' laughter as they run up to the house floats back to me, and the crickets' chorus fills the dusk.

Somewhere in the distance a coyote howls at the rising moon. We've finished feeding the animals. The goats are now secure in their stall, the hens are roosting in the little red coop, and the horses have resumed grazing in dawning moonlight.

I glance back toward the barn and see light under the door. In their hurry to return to the house, someone forgot to turn out the light. Retracing my steps, I open the door and flip the switch. But as I turn to leave, looking through the door frame out to the pasture, I see a flicker of light, then another and another: fireflies.

They dance among the horses in the twilight and spill into the barn, making the night sparkle. In the gentle silence, I hear the family of barn swallows as they settle into their nest for a quiet night.

A sweet-smelling breeze drifts, pleasant and cool, across my face. Like the breeze, a realization sweeps over me. Though this setting may not be perfect—the barn needs a new coat of paint, the doors creak and the fence could use tightening—the sights and sounds make everything feel right. For that moment, all is calm. I let it seep in. Slowly, I turn to go, carrying a reminder to see the beauty in every day the Lord gives us. Sometimes it's the wonder in the most ordinary moments that ministers to our hearts most.

Light flows from the windows of the house, beckoning me inside. I pause at the gate, glad that God has given us this beautiful farm life. There is nowhere I'd rather be. Good night, barnyard. Thank you for moments like this that fill my heart with peace.

FARMHOUSE FRIENDS

Constant companions Mercury and Sirius are unlikely but absolutely delightful pals.

DEBBIE GARCIA-BENGOCHEA HIGH SPRINGS, FLORIDA

Even though we may be different, that doesn't mean we can't be friends. That's the message of real-life best friends Mercury, a miniature therapy horse, and Sirius, his very fluffy canine companion.

Sirius is a Maremma sheepdog, an Italian livestock guardian breed. This hardy breed is usually solid white, but Sirius has a few black spots. When Sirius was 2 months old, Mercury was born on the farm. He has spots, too, and a pretty unusual color pattern—three white legs and one dark leg, one white ear and one dark ear. Mercury and Sirius became instant friends.

When Mercury trots into the farmhouse, Sirius is not far behind. With his tiny little hooves, Mercury needs to practice walking on different floor surfaces. Sirius has huge fluffy paws that look too big for his body; he needs to practice good indoor manners.

Together, Mercury and Sirius learn how to walk up and down steps, ride in a truck, and walk and stand on a lead.

Mercury works with Gentle Carousel Miniature Therapy Horses, one of the largest equine therapy programs in the world. These therapy horses comforted the survivors and first responders of the mass shootings at Sandy Hook Elementary School in Newtown, Connecticut; Emanuel African Methodist Episcopal Church in Charleston, South Carolina; and Pulse nightclub in Orlando, Florida. They helped the tornado survivors of Moore, Oklahoma; victims of fires in Gatlinburg, Tennessee; and families in the aftermath of Hurricane Irma. They visit thousands of patients in children's and veterans' hospitals each year. When Mercury goes to a hospital visit, Sirius waits on the porch for him to return.

The therapy horses of Gentle Carousel are very small miniature horses.

Maremmas are a large dog breed, so when Sirius and Mercury are both fully grown, they will be about the same size. And together they'll share a happy life on the farm as forever friends.

Mercury visits a school for story hour (top); best friends Sirius and Mercury spend happy days together on the farm (above).

A SPECIAL DELIVERY

Building a replica of a 1920s milk wagon helped a farming aficionado find hope after tragedy.

SUSAN TERRY BATTLE CREEK, MICHIGAN

rowing up in Battle Creek, Michigan, Larry Newman always wanted to live on a farm. Starting one after high school was just too expensive, so he chose to be an electrician. But his fascination with this simple, honest way of life never left him. Instead of planting rows, Larry became a collector and went to work restoring classic pieces of farming Americana.

Visit his workshop and you'll find an array of items: signs; cream separators; bottles, milk jars and cans; toy trucks; a gravity wagon; a circus wagon; farming tools; and tractors. Some he sells, some he keeps, and some he gives away to those who love farming history.

In 2016, Larry and his wife, Diana, lost their son, Todd, to cancer. As Larry worked through his grief, he realized he had to do something special in Todd's honor. He found that something while hunting for treasure at a local sale. The old horse-drawn milk wagon was in extreme disrepair. Once it delivered milk, but it was repurposed as a rabbit hutch!

Larry then began a fact-finding mission to learn more about the milk wagon he had come to own. The wagon held clues to its past. Larry discovered that the original owner was Lilliberk Farms, which was established in 1918 by one J.F. Berkheimer and his wife, Lillie, in nearby Homer.

The couple had 150 Holsteins, which they eventually exchanged for Guernseys. Lacking reliable refrigeration, they delivered farm-fresh milk quickly by horse-drawn wagon to customers' front

Larry (far left) shows off the collection in his workshop. Above: A draft horse team pulls the wagon along a country road.

porches for 12 cents a quart. When Larry removed the wagon's tin panels, he uncovered the slogans "Certified Milk" and "Save the Babies." The latter referred to the high infant mortality rate during the 1920s caused in part by bacteria found in milk (a "Pure Milk" campaign began to help prevent early childhood death).

Now that Larry had his wagon, which he took apart piece by piece to use as a pattern, as well as a wealth of information about milk delivery in the early part of the 20th century, constructing the replica of the Lilliberk Farms milk wagon began.

His old friend Dave Vandlen offered his help and his large wood workshop. Larry and Dave started Dec. 1, 2018, and they rolled out the finished product on April 1, 2019. The pals spent countless hours measuring, cutting, sanding, gluing and bolting pieces together to produce a showpiece that is now being enjoyed in towns all over southwestern Michigan.

The only original pieces on the milk wagon are the door handles; however, a considerable amount of history is also included in the finished product. World War I-era glass found at Fort Custer near

Battle Creek replaced the old windows. Larry found the 100-year-old steel wheels at Hansen Wheel and Wagon Shop in South Dakota. These were cleaned up and painted by KC's Collision in Bellevue, Michigan. Signs and Designs of Battle Creek provided the lettering and decals.

They replaced the original canvas roof with vinyl. Larry and Dave calculated they used 200 board feet of oak in the wagon as well as 5-by-5-foot panels of Russian birch.

Since finishing the milk wagon, Larry has spent many hours taking his most elaborate project to car and tractor shows and antique car museums. He had fun at the annual Cereal Festival parade in Battle Creek, where friends hitched their Percheron draft horses to pull the wagon along the parade route.

Especially poignant is the fact that his late son, Todd, is listed on the side of the wagon as the milkman. The circle is complete. What started as a tribute and a way to grieve the loss of a loved one has turned into something special for Larry. It has given him hope after tragedy and is leading to a host of new memories.

FARMING WAS HIS TRUE CALLING

B.J. Pigott never complained about working evenings and weekends, because to him, it wasn't work at all.

JOANN PIGOTT HOUSTON, TEXAS

My father, B.J. Pigott, retired after working more than 30 years for the New Orleans Furniture Co. in Columbia, Mississippi, but he was a farmer through and through.

He farmed all his life and was gifted at it, relying on knowledge, skill, intuition, the *Farmers' Almanac* and basic tools. He had to abandon school as a child and help out on his family's farm, and though he only had a fourth grade education, he was a very smart man.

After my father's shift ended at his day job, and on weekends, too, he'd come home and labor at his true passion. He would get up before sunrise on weekends and work in his field—in long sleeves and often in extreme heat—until nightfall. The only time he took a break was when it rained.

Not once did I hear him complain or say he was tired of farming, and it wasn't until I was an adult that I understood why.

He was doing what he loved. Farming was his true calling.

As children, we spent summer breaks helping our father plant and harvest crops that included peas, greens, squash, beans, okra, onions, corn, cucumbers, potatoes, peanuts, tomatoes and watermelon. We kept some, shared some with neighbors and sold some at market. We also raised cows, chickens, pigs and goats.

To be perfectly honest, we didn't like giving up our summer vacations every year and getting up before sunrise to go out into the fields. But a few years ago, I overheard my father talking to a neighbor. He said part of the reason he farmed was so he could keep his kids out of trouble. It certainly worked—after laboring outside, we were too tired to do anything else.

One spring, about a year before my father died, I took a trip back home to Sandy Hook, Mississippi. And there was Dad, in the field early in the morning, 88 years old, in long sleeves and playing tug of war with the hard, dry ground.

I am enormously proud that he could keep doing the work he loved until nearly the end of his life. And today, I would give just about anything for some of my father's homegrown vegetables.

Joann's dad, B.J., grew up farming and tended the land throughout his life, prioritizing it for himself and for his family.

Left: Mrs. Cates (at right) teaches art at the Opportunity Center. Right: Katie and Lori show off the dress Mrs. Cates made.

LESSONS OF LOVE

A chance meeting of a delightful friend leads to new skills, many smiles and a family's grateful thanks.

LORI SHELDON BORGER, TEXAS

Looking around the room of people selling crafts, jellies and baked goods at the arts and craft sale, I couldn't help smiling. I had been looking for something like this ever since we moved to our small town in northern Texas. I hoped that somewhere in this mix of people there was a new friend for my daughter Katie and for me.

After visiting numerous booths, we met Mrs. Cates, an older woman selling her artwork. She and Katie hit it off right away. I asked if she would teach Katie to draw, and she said, "Sure, and you both need to come visit me." We took her up on her offer and began a delightful friendship that still blesses our family 10 years later.

In addition to drawing lessons, Mrs. Cates has instructed Katie in painting, sewing, cooking, canning and other crafts. Mrs. Cates has taken my child under her wing as if she were Katie's aunt. When she was interested in sewing a fancy dress that was beyond her ability, Mrs. Cates sewed it for her. We are amazed at her care and understanding of a young girl's heart.

As Mrs. Cates has introduced us to more friends at the Opportunity Center, a senior citizens facility where she had been the director and still leads an art class, we have found she is as comfortable with older people as she is with children.

We were thrilled to learn she had been raised close to our former home in the South Texas countryside. She shared stories with us about her family's 36-acre farm. While her daddy served overseas during World War II, she helped run the farm. Mrs. Cates' early life wasn't all work; she had fun at family get-togethers packed with delicious homemade food.

Our family is so thankful for her influence. Mrs. Cates has attended many special occasions for Katie, and we have been there for her events as well, such as her 80th birthday celebration.

Over the years she has shared the gift of being herself in countless little ways. Many of the things she has shown us, we have shared with others—crafts, canning, sewing and, most of all, the joy of being a blessing to others.

The old hay barn on the farm.

CAREFREE COUNTRY DAYS

Life was simple and sweet at Mamaw and Papaw's.

CANDY THOMPSON KINGWOOD, WEST VIRGINIA

Memories of running through fields on my grandparents' farm as a child well up and embrace me like a soft blanket of comfort on days when the world can seem overwhelming.

I remember the old barns with haylofts to explore and jumping down from above into mounds of hay. I wandered the fields and found rocks to treasure, picked pretty wildflowers and chased butterflies, and lay down and watched clouds roll across the blue sky.

After plucking plenty of berries, I'd eat a few and then deliver the rest to Mamaw so she could make her delicious cobbler. I waded in the creek to catch minnows or tadpoles and skipped plenty of rocks—one, two or three times if you held your mouth just right.

In the evening darkness, I took great joy in catching lightning bugs in an old jar. I hiked up to the hayfield and counted the stars in the night sky, feeling lucky to see a random shooting star and to say hello to the man in the moon.

There were happy days riding on the old tractor or in the hay wagon. I chased chickens and gathered their eggs without getting pecked at. I picked apples in the orchard—juicy cherries, too, sweet and sour ones.

These are the memories money can't buy. I hope everyone gets the chance to experience the country in this way at least once in their lifetime. I will always cherish those innocent and carefree days, those simple times filled with joyful moments on Mamaw and Papaw's farm.

YOU CAN'T EAT JUST ONE

A family visit starts the Beals on a journey that leads to lots of peeled potatoes.

CAROLYN ANDERSON NEW ALEXANDRIA, PENNSYLVANIA

Before my great-grandparents John and Grace Beal moved to a farm in the 1940s, they lived in a town named Berlin, Pennsylvania.

A visit to Aunt Sadie introduced the Beals to a new way to make potatoes. Aunt Sadie sliced them very thin and quickly fried them in lard. She called them potato chips. The Beals had never had chips before, but they loved them! They couldn't wait to get home and try to make more of this delicious and unique family recipe.

At the start of the Great Depression in the early 1930s, the local coal mines closed and there was no work for John to support his family. The Beals thought that perhaps others would like potato chips as much as they did, and a business was born.

They purchased plenty of potatoes from local farmers. Grace and their daughter, Carmen, peeled about 400 pounds of them by hand. They soaked the potatoes in cold spring water to make them crisp before slicing them. They placed the slicer over the top of a lard can so the slices would fall right in. Each pass over the slicer produced four chips—also done by hand. Then they dried the slices before quickly frying them on an old coal-fired cookstove in the kitchen.

A special pan covered the entire stovetop. The stove lids were removed so the fire's heat would press right against the pan, which made the lard in the pan sizzling hot for frying. It took only a few short minutes in the hot lard to make chips. Grace removed the fried chips with a special wire mesh dipper and drained them, salted them and packed them into empty lard cans with a tight lid to keep the chips fresh and crispy.

John then stacked several filled cans in the car and delivered them in town to the local stores. Grocers scooped the chips out by hand and placed them into a brown paper bag that sold for 25 cents a pound.

In 1937, the new high school in Berlin opened and the school's snack bar sold Beal potato chips. The family continued producing chips until 1947, when Snyder's built a potato chip factory in Berlin, putting them out of business.

Eighty years ago snack foods were very scarce, and the Beals had no competition until Snyder's came to town. Today, when you walk down the grocery store's snack aisle, there are endless options of potato chip brands and flavors. Times sure have changed! But it's exciting to know my great-grandparents introduced in our corner of Pennsylvania something that would become an iconic snack.

John and Grace Beal made potato chips on their Pennsylvania farm.

COLORFUL CORNBREAD SALAD

PREP 30 min. **COOK** 15 min. + chilling
MAKES 14 servings

- 1 pkg. (8½ oz.) cornbread/muffin mix
- 1 cup mayonnaise
- ½ cup sour cream
- 1 envelope ranch salad dressing mix
- 1 to 2 Tbsp. adobo sauce from canned chipotle peppers
- 4 to 6 cups torn romaine
- 4 medium tomatoes, chopped
- 1 medium green pepper, chopped
- 1 medium onion, chopped
- 1 lb. bacon strips, cooked and crumbled
- 4 cups shredded cheddar cheese

1. Preheat oven to 400°. Prepare cornbread batter; pour into a greased 8-in. square baking pan. Bake until a toothpick inserted in the center comes out clean, 15-20 minutes. Cool completely in pan on a wire rack.

2. Coarsely crumble cornbread into a bowl. In a small bowl, mix mayonnaise, sour cream, salad dressing mix and adobo sauce.

3. In a 3-qt. trifle bowl or glass bowl, layer a third of cornbread, half of each of the remaining 6 ingredients, and mayonnaise mixture. Repeat layers. Top with the remaining cornbread and, if desired, extra chopped tomato and bacon. Refrigerate, covered, 2-4 hours before serving.

¾ CUP 407 cal., 31g fat (11g sat. fat), 61mg chol., 821mg sod., 18g carb. (6g sugars, 2g fiber), 14g pro.

CHERRY GRUNT

PREP 15 min. **COOK** 30 min.
MAKES 10 servings

- 1 can (16 oz.) pitted tart red cherries, undrained
- 1½ cup water
- ¾ cup sugar, divided
- ¼ cup butter, divided
- 1 cup all-purpose flour
- 1½ tsp. baking powder
  Pinch salt
- ⅓ cup 2% milk
- ½ tsp. vanilla extract

1. Place cherries and juice in a straight-sided skillet or Dutch oven along with water, ½ cup sugar and 2 Tbsp. butter. Simmer for 5 minutes.
2. Meanwhile, sift together flour, baking powder, salt and remaining sugar; place in a bowl. Cut in the remaining butter with a pastry blender. Add the milk and vanilla; stir to combine.
3. Drop by tablespoonfuls over cherry mixture. Cover and simmer until dumplings are cooked through, 20 minutes.

½ CUP 183 cal., 5g fat (3g sat. fat), 13mg chol., 128mg sod., 34g carb. (24g sugars, 1g fiber), 2g pro.

YELLOW SQUASH AND ZUCCHINI GRATIN

PREP 25 min. **BAKE** 10 min.
MAKES 6 servings

- 2 Tbsp. butter
- 2 medium zucchini, cut into ¼-in. slices
- 2 medium yellow summer squash, cut into ¼-in. slices
- 2 shallots, minced
- ½ tsp. sea salt
- ¼ tsp. coarsely ground pepper
- 4 garlic cloves, minced
- ½ cup heavy whipping cream
- 1 cup panko bread crumbs, divided
- ½ cup grated Parmesan cheese, divided

1. Preheat oven to 450°. In a large skillet, melt butter over medium heat; add zucchini, yellow squash and shallots. Sprinkle with the salt and pepper. Cook, stirring occasionally, until the zucchini and squash are crisp-tender, 4-6 minutes. Add garlic; cook 1 minute more.
2. Add the cream; cook until thickened, 3-5 minutes. Remove from heat; stir in ½ cup bread crumbs and ¼ cup cheese. Spoon mixture into a greased 11x7-in. or 2-qt. baking dish. Sprinkle with remaining bread crumbs and cheese. Bake until golden brown, 8-10 minutes.

1 CUP 203 cal., 14g fat (8g sat. fat), 39mg chol., 357mg sod., 15g carb. (4g sugars, 2g fiber), 6g pro.

HERBED FETA DIP

TAKES 25 min. **MAKES** 12 servings

- ½ cup packed fresh parsley sprigs
- ½ cup fresh mint leaves
- ½ cup olive oil
- 2 garlic cloves, peeled
- ½ tsp. pepper
- 4 cups (16 oz.) crumbled feta cheese
- 3 Tbsp. lemon juice
  Assorted fresh vegetables

In a food processor, combine the first 5 ingredients; cover and pulse until finely chopped. Add feta cheese and lemon juice; process until creamy. Serve with assorted vegetables.

¼ CUP 176 cal., 15g fat (5g sat. fat), 20mg chol., 361mg sod., 2g carb. (0 sugars, 1g fiber), 7g pro.

PICKLED BEET SALAD WITH BACON VINAIGRETTE

PREP 10 min. **COOK** 25 min.
MAKES 16 servings

- 8 cups fresh baby spinach
- 1 jar (16 oz.) pickled whole beets, drained and cut into wedges
- 1 small red onion, thinly sliced
- ½ cup sliced radishes
- 1 lb. bacon strips, chopped
- ⅓ cup cider vinegar
- 3 tsp. brown sugar
- 1½ tsp. Dijon mustard
- ½ tsp. pepper
- ¼ tsp. salt
- 1 cup crumbled goat cheese

1. In a large bowl, toss spinach, beets, and the onion and radish slices. Set aside.

2. In a large skillet, cook bacon over medium heat until crisp, stirring occasionally. Remove with a slotted spoon; drain on paper towels.

3. Add vinegar, brown sugar, mustard, pepper and salt to bacon drippings; bring to a boil. Drizzle the warm dressing over spinach and toss to coat. Sprinkle with goat cheese and bacon. Serve immediately.

1 CUP 165 cal., 13g fat (5g sat. fat), 27mg chol., 335mg sod., 7g carb. (5g sugars, 1g fiber), 5g pro.

VANILLA CREAM FRUIT TART

PREP 25 min. **BAKE** 25 min. + chilling
MAKES 12 servings

- ¾ cup butter, softened
- ½ cup confectioners' sugar
- 1½ cups all-purpose flour
- 1 pkg. (10 to 12 oz.) white baking chips, melted and cooled
- ¼ cup heavy whipping cream
- 1 pkg. (8 oz.) cream cheese, softened
- ½ cup pineapple juice
- ¼ cup sugar
- 1 Tbsp. cornstarch
- ½ tsp. lemon juice
- 1½ to 2 cups fresh strawberries, sliced
- 1 cup fresh blueberries
- 1 cup fresh raspberries

1. Preheat oven to 300°. Cream butter and confectioners' sugar until light and fluffy. Beat in flour (mixture will be crumbly). Pat onto a greased 12-in. pizza pan. Bake until lightly browned, 25-28 minutes. Cool.

2. Beat melted chips and cream until smooth. Beat in cream cheese until smooth. Spread over crust. Refrigerate 30 minutes. Meanwhile, in a small saucepan, combine the pineapple juice, granulated sugar, cornstarch and lemon juice. Bring to a boil over medium heat; cook and stir until mixture is thickened, about 2 minutes. Cool.

3. Arrange berries over cream cheese layer; brush with the pineapple mixture. Refrigerate 1 hour before serving.

1 PIECE 433 cal., 28g fat (17g sat. fat), 60mg chol., 174mg sod., 43g carb. (28g sugars, 2g fiber), 5g pro.

TURKEY SAUSAGE PIZZA

PREP 20 min. **BAKE** 15 min.
MAKES 8 servings

- 1   loaf (1 lb.) frozen bread dough, thawed
- ¾   lb. Italian turkey sausage links, casings removed
- ½   cup sliced onion
- ½   cup sliced fresh mushrooms
- ½   cup chopped green pepper
- ½   cup pizza sauce
- 2   cups shredded part-skim mozzarella cheese

1. Preheat oven to 400°. With greased fingers, press dough onto a 12-in. pizza pan coated with cooking spray. Prick dough thoroughly with a fork. Bake until lightly browned, 10-12 minutes.

2. In a large skillet, cook the sausage, onion, mushrooms and green pepper over medium heat until sausage is no longer pink, 6-8 minutes, breaking up sausage into crumbles; drain.

3. Spread crust with pizza sauce. Top with the sausage mixture; sprinkle with cheese. Bake until crust is golden brown and cheese is melted, 12-15 minutes longer.

1 SLICE 283 cal., 9g fat (4g sat. fat), 32mg chol., 668mg sod., 30g carb. (4g sugars, 3g fiber), 18g pro. **DIABETIC EXCHANGES** 2 starch, 2 lean meat, ½ fat.

SLOW-COOKER SALSA CHICKEN

PREP 15 min. **COOK** 3 hours
MAKES 4 servings

- 4 boneless skinless chicken breast halves (6 oz. each)
- 1 jar (16 oz.) salsa
- 1¾ cups frozen corn, thawed
- 1 can (15 oz.) pinto beans, rinsed and drained
- 1 can (15 oz.) no-salt-added black beans, rinsed and drained
- 1 can (10 oz.) diced tomatoes and green chiles, undrained
- 1 tsp. sugar
- ½ tsp. salt
- ¼ tsp. pepper
  Optional: Hot cooked rice, cubed avocado, chopped fresh tomato, sliced green onions and lime wedges

Place chicken in a 4- or 5-qt. slow cooker. Top with salsa, corn, beans, diced tomatoes and chiles, sugar, salt and pepper. Cook, covered, on low until a thermometer inserted in chicken reads 165°, 3-4 hours. Serve with optional ingredients as desired.

1 CHICKEN BREAST HALF WITH 1½ CUPS BEAN MIXTURE 470 cal., 6g fat (1g sat. fat), 94mg chol., 1270mg sod., 55g carb. (8g sugars, 11g fiber), 47g pro.

CHICKEN SWISS BUNDLES

PREP 30 min. **BAKE** 20 min.
MAKES 6 servings

- 1 small onion, finely chopped
- ½ cup sliced fresh mushrooms
- 1½ tsp. butter, melted
- 1 garlic clove, minced
- 1 cup cubed cooked chicken breast
- ½ cup chopped roasted sweet red peppers
- 1 Tbsp. honey mustard
- ¼ tsp. salt
- ¼ tsp. lemon-pepper seasoning
- ¼ tsp. Italian seasoning
- 2 cups shredded Swiss cheese
- 12 frozen bread dough dinner rolls, thawed
- 2 Tbsp. butter, melted

1. Preheat oven to 350°. In a large skillet, saute the onion and mushrooms in butter until tender. Add garlic; cook 1 minute longer. Add the chicken, peppers, mustard and seasonings; heat through. Remove from the heat; stir in cheese.

2. Flatten each roll into a 5-in. circle. Place ¼ cup chicken mixture in the center of each of 6 circles. Brush edges with water; top with remaining circles. Press edges with a fork to seal.

3. Place bundles on greased baking sheets; brush with melted butter. Bake until golden brown, 18-22 minutes. Cut the bundles in half to serve.

1 BUNDLE 434 cal., 20g fat (10g sat. fat), 64mg chol., 722mg sod., 40g carb. (5g sugars, 3g fiber), 24g pro.

Handcrafted

CREATE A FEELING OF HOME

FEEDSACK POTHOLDER

WHAT YOU'LL NEED

Vintage feedsack
1 yd. insulated thermal batting
1 yd. thin cotton batting
Coordinating thread
Extra-wide double-fold bias tape in coordinating color
Iron
Sewing machine

DIRECTIONS

1. Wash and dry sack. Remove seams and iron with steam.
2. Cut a 7-in. square from the feedsack's graphic design for front of potholder. Cut an 8-in. square from sacks for back. Cut a 7-in. square from both kinds of batting.
3. Layer 8-in.-square back fabric wrong side up, cotton batting, thermal batting and 7-in. front fabric right side up. Pin layers to hold in place and quilt together as desired on a sewing machine.
4. Baste ¼ in. from outer edge. Trim back layer to 7-in. square.
5. Round 3 corners using rim of a drinking glass to mark the curves, leaving top left corner square. Trim corners.
6. Starting at square corner, attach bias tape to back of the potholder, carefully stitching around curves. Stop stitching ½ in. from square corner and leave a 5-in. tail of tape for a hanging loop.
7. Fold tape to front and press. Pin in place. Edgestitch around tape. At final corner, stitch tail close to tape edge to end.
8. Trim tail to 4 in. and fold to back of potholder to create a loop. Stitch raw end in place.

FLOWER COLLAGE

WHAT YOU'LL NEED

Assorted fresh flowers
Parchment paper
Thick paper or card stock
Picture frame
Craft glue
Flower press or several
heavy books
Paintbrush

DIRECTIONS

1. Place flowers on sheet of parchment paper, taking care to not overlap blooms. Top with second sheet of paper.
2. Place florals in flower press or between pages of large heavy books. Tighten press according to directions. For books, close and place on top of one another, adding extra weight on top, if needed. Keep in press for 2 weeks.
3. Cut paper or card stock to fit inside frame.
4. Remove flowers from press; arrange on paper. Brush glue lightly on back of florals and press into place. Dry thoroughly.
5. Press your collage between parchment sheets for a few days before inserting in a frame.

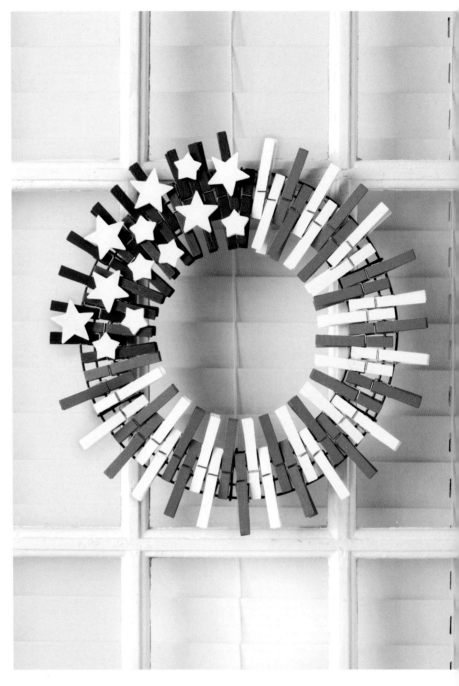

CLOTHESPIN WREATH

WHAT YOU'LL NEED

Standard-size clothespins
in red, white and blue
Wire wreath frame
Wood craft stars in various sizes
White craft paint
Paintbrush
Hot glue gun

DIRECTIONS

1. Clip blue clothespins on wire frame, alternating attaching from outside and inside. Fill about ¼ of wreath.
2. Clip red and white clothespins on frame in desired alternating pattern, filling entire frame and again alternating between outside and inside.
3. Paint stars white and allow to dry thoroughly.
4. Hot-glue stars into place on blue clothespins.

Fall's colors burn bright as a new day
begins in Arkansas' Upper Buffalo
River Wilderness Area.

Autumn

The Good Life

ROOM FOR ONE MORE

Our family's love for horses, goats and all kinds of animals helped write another chapter in the story of our farm.

ALLISON GESHINSKY WEST NEWTON, PENNSYLVANIA

Here on Windy Hills Farm near West Newton, fall is really, truly picturesque. The crisp, fresh air, blue skies, a patchwork of colors on the trees—it's the perfect autumn scene.

From my living room I see the hills ablaze in color, harvested fields and our two barns—built in 1860 and 1912—in a valley hidden from the main road. This is a farmer's version of a secret garden.

Our 145-acre farm has been in our family since the year 1948, when my great-grandparents Frank and Yadwiga Zima bought the place. They came from Poland in the 1920s with the dream of starting a dairy, and they raised their children on the land.

As my great-grandparents got older, they transitioned the farm to beef cattle and their sons looked for full-time jobs off the farm. When the cattle operation ended, they leased the land to crop farmers and the barns stood empty for many years.

The story of Windy Hills might have ended there, but our love for animals brought new life to the farm.

My sister, Sarah, and I grew up here and we had always wanted a horse—every

little girl's dream! In March 2004, that dream came true when my mother, JoAnne, came home from the grocery store with an ad for a horse for sale. I was 8 years old at the time and a little wary of large animals. We went to look at Daisy and she was a perfect match for us!

First, we had to find a place for her in the barn. It was just one horse, right? How much work could it be? It turned out to be our labor of love. With financial help from my grandparents Granny and Pappy Zima, we renovated one of the barns, which was filled with old equipment and cattle stanchions. We added a metal roof, painted, and got the barn ready for Daisy.

Well, as soon as we had one horse, Sarah and I wanted another. That's how the herd expanded. I had no idea that my affection for animals would grow each and every time we brought another into our hearts and home. As I became more at ease with these large creatures, we added goats to our flourishing farm family.

Everyone who visited fell in love with the place, as well as the care we gave to our animals. Windy Hills quickly became the go-to sanctuary for animals in need. We were given horses whose owners could no longer afford to board them, baby goats whose owners no longer had time to care for them, chickens whose owners were moving, and calves whose mothers had rejected them. At our farm, there's always room for one more.

What was once a run-down farm is now a fully functioning operation. Today we have over 40 dairy goats, 11 horses, beef cows and chickens. We sell eggs and goat's milk to help support the menagerie. We care for our animals, we grow corn, oats and soybeans, and we make hay to feed our herd of critters. My mom's dream is to have a certified dairy goat farm when she retires. I guess we'll see what the future has in store for our farm!

The farm was a wonderful place to be a country kid. Sarah and I spent our youth

Allison's family (above) turned the old farm (left) into a sanctuary for animals like her barrel racing horse Reba (top).

in 4-H showing barrel horses, mini horses, beef cows, dairy goats and dogs. In the beginning, we really had no idea what we were doing. However, as we grew, we learned more about our animals and became very successful with them. We've won many ribbons and trophies and made it to the state championship with our horses. My dairy goat, Lacey, even won Best Doe of Show at our county fair! The hard work and dedication we learned growing up on a farm has truly paid off.

Country scenery is a beautiful thing, but the land is so much more. It's the ground we grew up on. It's the hours of blood, sweat and tears that were poured into it. Loving the land and the animals residing on it has led to mental, emotional and physical transformations.

This farm is where we spent all night in the barn helping deliver baby goats, and all day playing with them. It's my heart and soul, my past, present and future, my life and my home.

Thanks to the hard work of my great-grandparents, we have a wonderful life here on the farm. And with the help of Granny and Pappy Zima, we were given the opportunity to preserve the farm not only for us, but for generations to come.

This rustic chicken coop (top), which is home to about 30 birds, has stood since the early 1900s. Kitty, a barn cat, lets curious kids get close (middle). In the spirit of the season, Allison and her family decorated these hay bales (above).

DEEP ROOTS

The homestead where memories were made still nourishes
this extended family.

ANN KENNEDY LIBERTY, MISSOURI

The road that leads to my late Aunt Beulah and Uncle Nobel's house, a place near and dear to my heart, is narrow, twisting, and lined with thick woods, blooming chicory, Queen Anne's lace and orange daylilies. Flowing in a black wave, the road is best traveled if you're the driver. Along the way we pass very small towns. We wonder how the local churches can survive, but on a Sunday morning, it is apparent they do. We see six cars at one, and nine cars at another—in towns with populations of under 100, that is significant. In sweet anticipation we pass through the dusty crossroads: Sassafrass Ridge, Velvet Antler and Justa Drive. And we wonder who came up with these quirky names deep in the Ozark foothills of Missouri.

With two front doors never used, the old house stands proudly tired on a ridge overlooking the pasture where I, as a kid, climbed over the fence, crossed the field and headed for the creek. I would wade and return with what appeared to be a small twist of bright red thread on my ankle, only to be told it was leeches. They didn't hurt. Dealing with leeches wasn't as bad as enduring the firm lecture about never crossing the pasture when the bull was there. Doing so was completely worth it. I found an arrowhead.

That old home is a beautiful and very meaningful spot, as is the house of my cousins, Jerry and Jeannette, across the road. Bordered by a blueberry patch, a big vegetable garden, beehives and lush, green fields, the open space there is better at accommodating our large group around the dining room table. Both places bring a special kind of gratitude.

I consider how fast time passes, wonder how my oldest cousin could be 90 years old and how I was ever bold enough to ignore a 2,000-pound bull. And I wonder about all the things that bind a family to land. As we walk out the door of the house, I look back and glimpse arrowheads, collected over the generations, now framed to help us all remember those earlier days.

Pastures surround Aunt Beulah and Uncle Nobel's former home (above), now owned by Ann Kennedy's cousins.

IN LOVE WITH MONTANA

Moving to Big Sky Country was a dream come true and a chance
to raise our children in harmony with the land.

MONICA SPENCER VICTOR, MONTANA

The rugged beauty of Montana's Bitterroot Valley is simply unfathomable.

Photographers and writers dream about it. Romantics long for it and adventurers crave it. The scenery whispers of the past and reminds us that a brighter future is on the horizon for those who aren't afraid to work for it.

The call to move out west came four years ago when my husband, John, who is a physical therapist assistant, got a job offer. We were living in Missouri at the time, but John had always wanted to be

a mountain man. I grew up in Washington state, surrounded by peaks. The move made sense.

Our home in Victor lies between the rolling tops of the Sapphire Mountains to the east and the jagged peaks of the Bitterroot Mountains to the west, with a patchwork of farms and ranches mixed along the foothills and the banks of the Bitterroot River. A few towns are scattered along the way.

The valley is roughly 25 miles at its widest point and 96 miles long, stretching from Lolo in the north to Lost Trail Pass

Dramatic skies hang overhead during fall (top). The Spencers count curious horses among their neighbors (above).

on the border with Idaho in the south. Our valley is overflowing with big sky views, jagged and rolling mountain landscapes, and the wild and scenic Bitterroot River, which cuts the valley in half.

We Montanans call our home "The Last Best Place," after an anthology of stories by the state's best writers. To live in such a beautiful region is a blessing. We rent our humble home and have amazing and generous landowners who let us treat this place as if it were our very own.

The 50-plus acres yield bountiful fruit and vast fields of grass. Our family enjoys the landscape, gardens, livestock, hunting and so much more. Vivid culture, a rich and deep history, abundant wildlife and tightknit communities surround us.

The horses share farm fields with the local herds of elk and deer. Occasionally we are lucky enough to spot a stray moose looking for willows to forage through. We even had a black bear break one of our van's windows when it was nosing around a while back!

In addition to my part-time work as a youth pastor, I home-school our five children: Alexander, 14, Abigaile, 12, Madison, 10, Gabriella, 8, and Amelia, 4. Raising them here is a privilege. This place provides a solid foundation upon which our children can grow and have freedom to roam. The mountains stand strong as if to protect them from the outside world. It is a haven for the weary soul, a place of refuge for the wanderer.

Our view of the mountains invites us to explore their beauty, mysteries and wild spirit. In the summer, the cool stillness of the night and the rhythmic sounds of crickets refresh our spirits, readying us for whatever we face in the days ahead.

The remnants of the hard work of past generations are visible all around us. We relish it today and work to make the land better for future generations.

Our children learn firsthand the importance of hard work when they help out with hauling hay in the summer, work in the garden or butcher a deer or elk they have harvested from this land. It gives them the understanding that nothing comes free and that sometimes, living well requires blood, sweat and tears. They're learning to appreciate the feeling of success that follows a hard day's work.

And, as a reward, we sit on our porch and watch the sun paint the mountains and sky with vivid pinks, purples, blues and oranges as day gives way to night.

In his 1962 book *Travels with Charley: In Search of America*, John Steinbeck wrote, "I am in love with Montana. For other states I have admiration, respect, recognition, even some affection, but with Montana it is love, and it's difficult to analyze love when you are in it."

We wholeheartedly agree.

Montanans call our home 'The Last Best Place.'"

The freedom to roam brought the Spencers (clockwise from left: Abigaile, Alexander, Gabriella, Amelia, John, Madison and Monica) to Montana, where the children help haul hay (top right) and explore nature (top left).

Gage Richard goes for the proverbial gold (left); men lead a wagon of corn to the scales.

HUSK ON!

An annual competition brings together folks of all ages.

LOIS HOFFMAN SHERWOOD, MICHIGAN

More than 3 inches of rain fell, and there was mud everywhere. Horses and wagons, people and tractors trudged through deep gullies. As the day wore on, it only got muddier. Still they came, young and old—to husk.

This was my third year at the Indiana State Corn Husking Contest. The first year, I went out of curiosity. I remembered hand-husking corn as a kid to open up the fields so Dad could get his corn picker in without knocking any of the crop down.

Initially, I wanted to try my hand at the contest and see what kinds of memories it might bring. In the end, I met a lot of nice people, had fun and felt I was helping to preserve a bit of history.

Husking contests first gained popularity in the early 1900s, when communities more regularly gathered to harvest corn by hand. Soon, competitions in husking began cropping up. They blossomed into state and national events, and tens of thousands came to watch. The winners became well known.

"We are trying to preserve the history and traditions of farming that are being lost," says Clay Geyer, president of the Indiana Corn Husking Association. "Our goal is for everyone to understand where their food comes from and how it's produced." Indiana's annual contest began in 1926, and Clay competed for the first time in 2009. Nine states—Illinois, Iowa, Minnesota, Kansas, Missouri, Nebraska, Ohio, South Dakota and Indiana—hold annual competitions, and the nationals rotate among them.

As Clay will tell you, the work required to pull an event off goes on year-round. He

Melanie Gebhart catches a ride to the scales (top). A contest judge and the gleaner follow a corn husker (above).

assigned row, as well as any ears that miss the wagon. Methods vary: Some huskers go as fast as they can to get more total poundage, and they don't worry about husking clean. Other contestants are more methodical in their approach.

The contest has no age barriers, and young and old alike turn out to try their hand. Folks from 2 to 92 can be found at the Indiana event, and they come out year after year, for all sorts of reasons.

Gage Richard, age 13, has husked in the state competition for four years and has been to nationals twice. Marshall Finke, a friend of his, has been husking for three years. Both were essentially born into the event, thanks to their granddads.

Gage's grandfather Ted Richard has taken part in nationals four times, and he won his category in 2016. And Marshall's grandfather Jerry Calloway brings a team of draft horses every year. His horses pull some of the wagons the huskers toss corn into, and they are as seasoned as the contestants. "Lots of people come to see the horses," Jerry says. "It reminds them of the old days."

Sophia and Melanie Gebhart came back this year with their grandfather Robert Hamilton. Robert's family grows and mills their own specialty cornmeal, and while his granddaughters participate in the contest, they also come to hang out and spend time with him.

There were others, too, whose stories touched my heart. The first husker of the day was a woman named Janice Hurford. With a tear in her eye, she told me, "My dad won the state contest years ago and ever since then this has been on my bucket list. It was just time."

Charlotte Triplet, 3 years old, was one of the smallest supporters. She was a bit too young to husk, but her dad, Zach Triplet, is vice president of the Indiana Corn Husking Association and her mother, Emily Porman, is the secretary. They brought her along to see what it was all about, reasoning that one is never too young to learn.

This contest is about so much more than husking—it's about remembering the old ways, making friends and enjoying a fun, wholesome day with other farmers. Sure, curiosity brought me here, but everything else keeps me coming back.

meets with business owners, develops partnerships and does promotional work at fairs, other contests and farm shows throughout the year. And he arranges with farmers across the state to help plant and manage a corn crop at his farm that will be ready in time for contest day.

The competition starts with a cornfield divided into sections. Participants choose the sections and rows they want to shuck. They have a set number of minutes, based on the class they're in, to see how many pounds of corn they can husk and toss into a wagon.

A judge and a gleaner follow each of the contestants. The judge times the husker and the gleaner carries a bag to pick up all the corn the contestant misses on their

PATCH WORK

This former farm kid started small, but it wasn't long before he returned to his roots.

MICHAEL J. LARSON WHEATON, MINNESOTA

Growing up on a farm, I loved every aspect of farming life. Well...maybe not removing manure from the chicken house, but pretty much everything else.

In college, I studied to become a high school science teacher. But in 42 years of teaching, I couldn't get farm life out of my system. So I stayed connected to the soil by cultivating a large home garden.

With three children, my wife and I decided to plant pumpkins. In the early years, we grew just enough to satisfy our family's Halloween needs. But each season saw an increase in the number of pumpkin hills, and it wasn't long before I grew more of those big orange orbs than the family could use. It was clear we needed to find new homes for the surplus.

After one exhausting season of trying to disperse the excess crop, it occurred to me that a Pumpkins For Sale sign might help us whittle down the pumpkin population. To my happy surprise, cars began pulling off the road to buy our extra supply. That first year, sales fetched us an extra $150. Not bad! The following season, I ordered more seeds than usual. Over the next few years, the pattern continued and sales kept climbing.

The workload increased as well. New ground had to be broken up to make more pumpkin hills, and every two years, I had to locate, collect and spread manure over the field to maintain healthy soil.

Families brought cameras along to record their visits to the pumpkin patch, and I responded by building a backdrop with straw bales and a corn shock where guests could gather for pictures.

Twenty years ago, our annual sales consisted of several dozen gourds. By last autumn, we were growing, displaying and selling more than 1,600 pumpkins. What started as a hobby became a business.

If you ask me what the most satisfying thing about having a pumpkin patch was, it wouldn't be the money (although for a retired guy like me, that was much appreciated). What I liked best was the children's laughter rising into the air as they romped among the pumpkins, straw bales and corn shocks.

But then, like the Kenny Rogers song says, you've got to know when to fold 'em—and it got to the point where planting 450 hills, weeding, handling insect control and lugging 25-pound gourds around at harvesttime was taking a toll. Last fall I made the decision, letting customers know that I would be retiring.

This spring I seeded the old pumpkin gardens with native prairie grasses and wildflowers. Happy children will be replaced by happy pollen-gathering bees. My pumpkin-growing practice has come to an end, but I'll never forget it.

Now, I wonder how difficult it would be to learn the art of beekeeping.

Michael Larson examines one of the big orange fruits of his labor.

Scrapbook

1

2

1. AUTUMN FEAST
I always enjoy my backyard birds. One of my favorite things is setting up scenes for them to visit. They will come if I just put out food. This Carolina chickadee stopped by to grab a snack.

JACQUELINE HODSDON FOREST, VIRGINIA

2. A BUSHEL AND A PECK
Cousins Abigail and Bryce had a great time during their first apple-picking experience with my daughter, Laikley. I'm sure they will return to the orchard for years to come!

CHARITY HOUGH XENIA, ILLINOIS

1. GLORIOUS MORNING

As I walked down to the pasture to help my dad with some chores on an early foggy morning in October, I stopped to watch him walk through the gate. Dad paused for a minute so I could snap this photo of him.

PAMELA DAVIS NEW CONCORD, OHIO

2. PUMPKIN PICKERS

My husband's brother plants pumpkins at our farm every year, and he always needs help harvesting. Our crew usually consists of the adults and quite a few grandchildren.

DAWN GREEN GRAND MOUND, IOWA

3. FARM'S BEST FRIENDS

These four-legged friends never hesitate to help out at the farm, and they're very popular on social media, too.

CASSANDRA KNEPSHIELD
VANDERGRIFT, PENNSYLVANIA

1

1. EVERYBODY PILE ON!

We had a happy visitor in the leaf pile with my kids Hannah and Mason—our adorable fur baby KitKat, who loves jumping and playing in the leaves just as much as the kids do.

CHRISTY WARDEN FLORIEN, LOUISIANA

2. ARE YOU MY DAD?

My son, Carson, tries intently to figure out just who this guy is at the local pumpkin patch.

MAEGAN STAUFFER FINDLAY, OHIO

3. NATURE'S BEAUTY

The sun felt so warm in Zion National Park as its rays shone through the brilliant yellow leaves. We walked the bridge to get across the river below.

MARIBETH ROCKE SECOR, ILLINOIS

2

3

A BREATHTAKING SIGHT
After an arduous trek through Vermont with a hiking group, we felt we needed a little "down time." One of my hiking comrades knew how to use the time wisely.

WENDY HARRISON SAN DIEGO, CALIFORNIA

1. JUST THE RIGHT SIZE

We visited Bishop's Orchards in Guilford, Connecticut, a gigantic property with a pumpkin patch. Ben got to pick out his own special little pumpkin.

KRISTA KNUDSON NEW HAVEN, CONNECTICUT

2. ACTION SHOT

I was about to snap a photo of the maple tree in all its fall glory when a gust of wind created a confetti-like atmosphere that mirrored being right on the middle of a ticker-tape parade.

DWAYNE BUTLER LISBON, WISCONSIN

3. MAKING FRIENDS

I discovered a group of joyful horses down my country road. This horse and I have a special bond. Whenever I need someone to just be there, I can visit these horses just a short walk away.

MELANIE BEILNER FERNDALE, WASHINGTON

1. CAUSE FOR CELEBRATION
Coraletta and Jim celebrate their 50th anniversary on the Greenbrier Trail, which winds through a few tunnels and past the occasional horse-drawn wagon.

CORALETTA HOUCK
PARKERSBURG, WEST VIRGINIA

2. HARVESTING ART
During this season, we are surrounded by glorious artwork that only Mother Nature can create. This is my brother Mark Speltz during a past fall harvest.

JULIE KALMES ROLLINGSTONE, MINNESOTA

3. REGAL EAGLE
I stopped at the Ashokan Reservoir in New York with my wife and 4-month-old son. The scenery was fantastic even on a cloudy day. While we spent most of our time taking photos of foliage, we lucked out when we found this very cooperative bald eagle sitting in a pine tree along the walking path. It's the closest any of us have gotten to an eagle in the wild.

PHILLIP WERMAN NEW YORK, NEW YORK

1. HIDDEN GEM

After many years of visiting this area near Old Fort, North Carolina, where my dear grandparents lived, I finally saw this beautiful waterfall with my own eyes. It was also the first trail I ever hiked alone, and the last time autumn colors gleamed before the rains came.

SAMANTHA MICHAEL
SPARTANBURG, SOUTH CAROLINA

2. AUTUMN'S WELCOME MAT

I am mesmerized by nature's beauty and thankful to see, smell and feel each gorgeous day while welcoming friends, animals and wildlife to our little piece of heaven.

ANGELA DUBIVSKY SOMERSET, NEW JERSEY

3. EW, COOTIES!

My twin siblings, Kayana and Karson, keep us all entertained! They delight in playing together, and Karson loves teasing his sister. But it looks as if Karson isn't really into a hug.

MICHELLE MARTIN PLYMOUTH, OHIO

1. HILLSIDE HISTORY
It was a splendid fall day in the Colorado Rockies when I happened across the abandoned Gilman zinc mine and company town at Minturn, Colorado.

ARNOLD BAUMFALK ST. HELENS, OREGON

2. FALL COLORS
It's easy to find peace and contentment after a long day by watching beautiful horses in the setting sun.

TAYLOR OLSON CASA RIO, SASKATCHEWAN

3. KNEE-HIGH AND SMILING
My husband, Clay, and our son, Charles, pause amid the field corn. We also grow soybeans and raise cattle. We're happy to be bringing Charles up on the farm, living the country life!

HOPE CHESSER GOSPORT, INDIANA

Heart & Soul

HELPING HANDS

Grassroots relief haulers bring supplies, and a little bit of hope, to farms in need.

HEATHER QUINN

T he farmer and his hogs...of all the things Brittany Hamlin saw in Iowa and Nebraska this past spring, that is the memory that stands out. Brittany is a co-founder of the Ohio Relief Haulers, a charitable organization that provided assistance to farmers during the 2019 floods. This particular farmer's land was still underwater when she arrived with her group. On his fields she saw cattle standing belly-deep in mud and water. She asked him how many he had lost, and he said just a few.

"We're doing pretty good on the cattle end," he told Brittany as she and their crew unloaded hay and other supplies. "But we're going to have to start over on our hog end." Of more than 900 hogs, he and his family had been able to save only about 60, most of them piglets.

"It was a son and a father running this ranch," Brittany recalls. "The son turned to me and said, 'My dad was throwing as many piglets as he could in the trailer before it filled with water. I finally turned around, grabbed my dad by the coattails and said, "We gotta go! I'm not losing you, too!"' They had water up to their waists by the time they pulled out of their farm with the handful of pigs that they had saved."

Like so many others, their losses were devastating. But when Brittany visited the farmer again a few weeks later during a second relief trip to the area, he was hopeful, already looking to the future.

Hope. That's what Brittany says the Ohio Relief Haulers bring, delivering hay, fencing, humanitarian supplies and much more. This spring, hope came in the form of volunteers driving 82 trucks full of hay, feed, fencing, and medical and veterinary supplies to more than 20 locations around Iowa, Nebraska and Missouri.

STARTING FROM SCRATCH

Brittany founded the Ohio Relief Haulers with her husband, Travis Hamlin, in 2017. At that time, wildfires across Oklahoma, Kansas and Texas were wreaking havoc on farmers. The couple, looking for a way to help, learned about a small group that was bringing relief to the region, but it was too late to join. So they decided they would go on their own.

Brittany created a page on Facebook that she shared with local farmers and others, and Ohio Relief Haulers was born. Their first trip was a success—a convoy of 52 trucks joined them, all full of supplies donated by farmers or local businesses.

"It was all just spread by word-of-mouth," Brittany says. "We didn't pay for any of the items or any advertising. We just contacted local companies and made connections with different feed and

> " They literally lost everything, and they're still planning on how they can save it."

fencing dealers and asked, 'Do you have anything extra that you're willing to donate or spare?'"

There were a lot of folks in need this past spring. A protracted winter kept snow on the ground longer than usual, preventing many farmers from unloading their grain bins. A mid-March warmup led to rivers, particularly the Missouri, being inundated with meltwater and rain.

Across the Midwest, farms and towns were overwhelmed by floodwaters. Worst hit were the areas around the Missouri River in Iowa and Nebraska, with at least $3 billion in property damage estimates in just those states. Many of those losses were to farms.

Ag Community Relief volunteer Austin Rossen stacks bales at a Nebraska drop point (left). Above: an Ohio Relief Haulers convoy; Travis and Brittany (in red tank top) with fellow volunteers.

MANY HANDS MAKE LIGHTER WORK

As soon as the floods began, Ohio Relief Haulers got to work. With the help of Ag Community Relief, a Michigan-based group that organizes relief convoys for farmers, Brittany and Travis started to organize two trips to affected areas. As before, they posted on their Facebook page, inviting community members to donate supplies and volunteer to drive. They went out on April 5 and April 26, with 52 trucks on the first trip and 30 on the second.

This was a huge organizational feat on behalf of the Relief Haulers, but what made it possible was cooperation from end to end—from those willing to donate or volunteer their time, to coordinators in flood-hit regions working to make sure supplies reached the farmers who needed them most.

In Sidney, Iowa, Dustin Sheldon was on the receiving end of donations for farmers around the southwestern corner of his state. A farmer himself, as well as a Fremont County supervisor, Dustin had seen floods and other natural disasters before, but he was more accustomed to being on the giving end of the assistance.

When floods swept the region in 2011, his brother's farm and home—the one

their grandfather once lived in—was underwater. But that same year, wildfires burned across western Texas, and he sent fencing supplies and hay to farmers there. When farmers in Montana were hit with wildfires from 2016 to 2017, his family farm sent two loads of hay to ranches out there. This was his first time receiving help; he says the experience was moving.

"The Ohio Relief Haulers have been—I can't even begin to explain the magnitude of what they've done for our community," Dustin says. "The amount of people that they've helped, the amount of money they raised and got donated...and the people that have donated their time and their transportation to get all the stuff here—it's really, really humbling for me."

Brittany says Dustin was instrumental in getting trucks and supplies where they needed to go, and that whenever haulers made drops in the area, he would come out to meet the volunteers, shake hands and say thank you. He volunteered his own equipment to unload supplies at the drop sites, and he even used a building on his property to store relief goods. He did all of this while his own family's farm was badly hit by flooding.

As Dustin says, helping other farmers out is just what farmers do.

Sarah Anthony and Larry Cooper, who offered their Verdigre Stockyards as a drop point for supplies landing in Nebraska, toss hay to an Ag Community Relief volunteer.

LEFT: FARM NEWS MEDIA/MICHIGAN FARM BUREAU; RIGHT: OHIO RELIEF HAULERS (2)

"These are guys that I work with. I see them very frequently," he says. "Farming is a passion, it's not just what you do to make a living. Agriculture's not a job where you enjoy being successful while someone else suffers—that's just not how it works. These are friends of mine, and neighbors."

SOURCES OF HOPE

Dustin emphasizes that help came from many places, from individuals and large groups alike. For example, the pilots who own and operate Cedar Ridge Aviation in Knox City, Texas—a company that offers spraying services in Iowa—flew up in one of their helicopters, provided aerial photography and took farmers up to see their land, all free of charge.

The Iowa Corn Growers Association donated goods, as did the Cattlemen's Association in that state.

Dustin's wife, Rhonda, has family in Texas who organized a private drive, hauling humanitarian supplies to the region. And he says there are many other groups that stepped in and helped, in the Fremont County area and across all of the states hit by the flooding.

As Dustin, Brittany and Travis know all too well, there is still much to be done before the worst-hit areas can completely recover. Many farms lost not only their ability to plant this year, but also grains stored in their bins from the previous year's harvest; these are massive losses not covered by crop insurance. But Dustin says that for him, walking away is not an option.

"I was born and raised in that bottom over there," he says. "My folks still live there today. I farmed that ground with my grandpa when I was a little kid. That's what we knew, and that's what we do. We farm, we raise cattle. And you want to be able to do what you do best. That's what everybody over here does. It's not just as simple as, 'We'll just sell it and move.' That's not really an option."

Thinking back to the farmer and his hogs, Brittany says, "They literally lost everything, and they're still planning on how they can save it. If I lost everything like that, I don't know if I could come back. But that little bit of hope that we hauled out there, it sparked."

From top: The group sends hay bales out on the road in style; Ohio Relief Haulers volunteers loaded fencing for transport to farms in need; many folks volunteered time, equipment and supplies to help Ohio Relief Haulers get the job done.

GROWING A FAMILY

Kind hearts and farm chores create a loving environment for three girls.

BETHANY BANKS ELIZABETHTON, TENNESSEE

F olks say that roots run deep on family ground, and nowhere is that truth more evident than in the Tennessee mountains where we live. Even the road signs bear the last names of families who have lived on this ground for the past 200 years. But our journey here and family story is a far cry from theirs.

My husband, David, and I purchased land here right after we got married. We are several generations removed from farming in our respective families, but the pull to return was strong. This little acreage and old house gave life to our farming dreams. We founded Free Reign Farm and learned to raise goats, plant gardens and make goat's milk soap. We loved the life and began to dream of sharing the bounty of country living with the next generation. But our story was about to take a twist.

For reasons that only God may ever understand, our longed-for pregnancy didn't come. The empty bedrooms in our farmhouse called to be filled, even as the ache in our hearts grew deeper. After much prayer, we found ourselves drawn to foster care. Here was a place where the blessings of farm life were needed more than any other.

Not long after that, three girls came into our lives. They were scared of everything. They hated the food, the animals and the dirt. They wouldn't play outside; instead they huddled on the steps, stubbornly refusing to take part in family activities.

We just kept living the life, working the land and inviting them in every day, and I watched God work miracles through the

experience of farm living. Before long, the children wanted to help plant the garden. Milking the goats with Mom became highly prized time—even worth fighting over. The kids learned not only to enjoy the food, but also to grow it, cook it and preserve it.

Cold winter snowstorms built character as they walked with us to feed hungry animals. Hailstorms taught empathy as they cried with us over ruined crops. Baby goats restored hope as the girls rejoiced with us over a new birth. Together, we became a family on this farm long before the adoption papers made it official.

Time marched on, and again I sat holding another pregnancy test, bracing myself for disappointment. I looked at the test in my hand and froze. Tears flooded my eyes as I sobbed with joy.

A few weeks later we broke the news to the girls, a little nervous about what they might think or feel. This new baby could really rock their boat. Would they feel unwanted? Would they think we didn't love them the same? Could we handle all this?

We called a family meeting. "Girls, we have something to tell you." Three girls stared back. "We're going to have a baby."

I watched huge smiles break across their faces. The oldest, Colleen, piped up,

"We know." David and I glanced at each other. "What do you mean, you 'know'?" I asked.

"We all got together and prayed for a baby brother," our daughter Georgia said triumphantly. "God's just delivering him."

We all welcomed the much-prayed-for baby months later. Sure enough, it was a boy. We named him Samuel, which means "asked of God." If ever a child was asked for, this one certainly was. Far from driving wedges in the family, the blessing of answered prayers knit us all together even tighter.

Though I never would have chosen to make a family this way, God knew best. If not for years of infertility, I might not have waded into fostering. I could have missed watching broken lives heal. This family might never have seen three sweet prayers for a baby brother answered with the miracle of an "impossible" pregnancy.

Our last name may never be on the road sign. We may not be able to pass on this place as "family ground," but nothing can take away the inheritance of values that were grown here. Those virtues will be around long after the house crumbles. God used this country home to provide roots, purpose, meaning and stability to children who were once lost.

Far left: The Banks family celebrates adoption day on the courthouse steps with daughters Colleen, Georgia and Caroline; miracle baby Samuel. Above: Tending to goats is a daily activity on Free Reign Farm.

SCHOOL MASCOT

An abandoned kitten becomes the teacher's pet
and makes reading fun.

DODIE EYER CLINTON, BRITISH COLUMBIA

I was the teacher at Big Bar School in the mountains of south-central British Columbia, miles away from the nearest small town. One day I was there working late with my two youngest children, my daughter Chia and son Jesse, who were also my students. Chia saw a car pull up to the school fence. Someone flung a tiny kitten over the fence and then sped off. Chia rushed outside and brought him in.

He was a black-and-white male, maybe 3 months old. He was squealing in terror. We petted him, gradually calming him down, and gave him some water and fed him a hot dog—the only thing we could find in the school refrigerator—which he eagerly gobbled up.

We made a bed out of an old quilt and set up a litter box for him in the bathroom. This was not the first time a cat had been at Big Bar School, so we were a little prepared. My first thought was that this feline might be a blessing in disguise.

The students were thrilled to find a tiny kitten in our school. We named him Moggy, and he loved all the attention. He could make a child feel special just by jumping onto his or her desk and curling up on the work in progress. Then I'd get the excuse, "I can't do my math because Moggy's lying on my book." Every day I read aloud to the kids. Moggy would sit on my lap and lend his deep, vibrating purr to my voice.

When one of my students was struggling to learn to read, I came up with the idea of making a simple book about Moggy to help the little boy. That turned out to be a hit, so I made a sequel. Ultimately, I created 12 Moggy books.

In Moggy's book life, he was friends with Willy the Squirrel, who owned a hot air balloon. His best pal was an elephant and he went skiing and had many other adventures. As the stories piled up, all the students became interested in the newest Moggy book and his next incredible, exciting escapade.

In everyday life, Moggy was part of each event at Big Bar School, from Christmas concerts to school pictures. He even came when his name was called, as a dog does.

One afternoon in June, I was reading aloud. All the kids were silent, intent on the story. Through the doors strolled Moggy with a writhing garter snake in his mouth. Somebody shouted, "Snake!" Pandemonium ensued. Frightened by the commotion, Moggy bolted away into the bathroom with his prize. The boys chased; girls screamed. I grabbed the snake from the cat and flung it out into the grass. It was a while before the dust settled.

Moggy lived with us at Big Bar School for more than 10 years. He spent summer holidays with my family, living in our barn with our cat, Frodo. In September he'd go back to school and work his magic on the kids. He was a cat with a lot of character and charm. Without a doubt, the students who passed through Big Bar School during the Moggy years will never forget him.

Moggy posed for pictures at Big Bar School.

Warren (right) bonded with his fellow veterans as they climbed to Georgia Pass.

THE HARDEST CLIMB

On the rocky cliffs of a Colorado peak, a group of wounded warriors discover the soothing powers of nature.

WARREN VAN OVERBEKE SHELBY, MICHIGAN

In 2017, a year after a medical discharge from the Air Force and after years of treatment for post-traumatic stress disorder, I felt restless. I wanted something to challenge me physically and psychologically. Then I found No Barriers Warriors, a program that helps veterans with disabilities experience the outdoors at no charge.

Erik Weihenmayer, the first blind person to summit Mount Everest, co-founded the program, which offers many different options depending on a person's physical abilities. I was selected to climb the 13,370-foot Mount Guyot in Colorado. I was ecstatic, but also afraid because I wouldn't be able to bring my wife, Leanne, or my service dog, Aniko. I was worried that no one would notice when I was struggling, as Leanne could, or bring me back from "over there" like Aniko did. But when I arrived in Denver and was introduced to the No Barriers Warriors staff and the other vets, I felt at ease. It was refreshing to be around others like me.

That afternoon we were driven to the small town of Frisco, where we spent the night after staff provided gear and taught us basic climbing skills. The next morning I walked out of the hotel, gear in hand, to one of the vans awaiting our team.

The mountains towering over us were so close that a brisk wind from the peaks chilled the morning air and sent shivers down my spine. A deep breath of the cool air filled my lungs and soothed my fears.

After an extended drive, we reached the trailhead, grabbed our gear and set off into the woods. Along the way we got to know one another as we shared our stories. During the ascent we overcame physical and psychological hurdles, which drew us closer. We were near the summit when the guides told us that the amount of snow atop Mount Guyot was too deep and unstable for our group to safely climb.

Though we were disappointed, we forged on to Georgia Pass, which sits near the Continental Divide in Mount Guyot's shadow. Atop Georgia Pass, the air was thin and the temperature frigid. The wind hummed a soft melody as it blew over the little vegetation that clung to the rocky surface. In that spot, 10 warriors and four team leaders gathered in celebration. We didn't reach the intended peak, but we had found a place of comfort and contentment.

It was clear to me that by the grace of God I was alive—I had made the journey, conquered what part of the mountain I could, and I was still standing. I couldn't have done it without my team's support.

Sun rays filter through the trees, tempting all would-be climbers.

A TREE TO CLIMB

My siblings made it to the top. Now it was my turn.

ELINOR DEWIRE CANTERBURY, CONNECTICUT

The tall, majestic tree stood on the lawn of my childhood home in Maryland. A tire swing hung from one branch and a knotted climbing rope hung from another. Boards nailed to the trunk served as a makeshift ladder.

As the youngest of eight kids, I was afraid to climb very high in that old tree. I was 6, and my arms and legs were too short to reach from limb to limb. The swaying branches in a stiff breeze made me shudder, and the bark felt scratchy and rough, except where foot traffic had worn it smooth. Still, I often watched with envy as my older siblings clambered far up to the top of the tree where the smallest branches waltzed with the wind. I tried to follow but quickly gave up. My older brothers teased me about my fears.

My sister, age 10, could climb the tree. She told me there were amazing things to see at its top. "I can't really describe it," she said. "You'll have to climb up and see for yourself."

Every day that summer I tried to reach the top, but I could barely make it halfway up the tree.

September came and the walnut tree was forgotten as books and papers and classmates occupied my time. I barely noticed the leaves turning yellow. By late October they lay scattered on the ground.

Then one Saturday in November, after we finished raking leaves and dumping them in a wooden compost bin, I stood alone beneath the tree. Without even thinking, I swung myself up on a limb and looked skyward.

"I can get to the top," I said to myself. "I know I can."

Up I scrambled, ignoring my weak arms, too-short legs and the ground below, not concerned with swaying branches or rough bark. I kept reaching and stepping, limb after limb, until the skinny, twiggy branches were the only ones left. Finally, I reached the top!

I wrapped my arms around a limb and let my legs dangle. The chilly wind whistling past made the treetop sway. I held on tightly, smiling. "This is not so scary after all," I said to myself, clutching the trunk and trembling just a little.

I looked upward and saw puffy clouds drifting against the powder blue sky. It seemed that I could almost reach up and touch them. To the west, rays of afternoon sun fanned over a cloud in spokes of golden light. I felt as if I had climbed into the heavens, and I fancied myself an angel, seeing the world from far above.

It was all so new, so marvelous, so exhilarating! I inhaled deeply, brave enough now to peer down through the lattice of limbs to the ground below. My sister was right, I thought. There were amazing things to see at the top of that old walnut tree.

THYE-WEE GN/SHUTTERSTOCK

THE FARM SCHOOL

Grandpa's pumpkin side business taught me to add,
subtract and save.

JIM BECK SEMINOLE, FLORIDA

My experience with pumpkins began on a warm day in the spring of 1946. We lived on 2 acres of land, part of my grandparents' farm. I loved the place. From the time I rolled out of bed in the morning until Mom called me home for supper, I served as Grandpa's shadow.

One spring day, Grandpa arrived at our back door on his tractor to take me to plant pumpkins. With me sitting on his lap, he drove the tractor, a little gray and red Ford 8N, to the field where he had planted corn. Grandpa had with him a brown paper bag full of large flat seeds, along with some fertilizer and a hoe. We drove across the head row to a strip of bare land. Grandpa had left a bit of the farm for me.

I followed him until he stopped. Using his hoe, he scratched a flat place in the dirt. Next he placed five seeds on the soil in a pattern to form a square. He counted, "One, two, three, four." And then the last one, "five," right in the center. He covered the seeds with a thin layer of dirt, creating a hill. Next he sprinkled a handful of fertilizer over the hill and used the hoe to scratch a bit more dirt on top of it. Then came the fun part! He told me to jump up and down on the hill to pack the seeds into the dirt. That was the beginning of my career in pumpkin farming.

A few days later, Grandpa and I found the seeds had burst through the ground. Then one afternoon it was time to thin the plants. Off we went to the field where I removed the two smallest seedlings from each hill. I had learned to subtract.

On a bright and chilly day in October, Grandpa hitched a hay wagon to the back of the tractor. Dad and I climbed aboard, and off we went to pick the pumpkins.

The next day I helped Grandpa sell them. We set up a card table upon which he placed a red coffee can that contained several coins and a few dollar bills.

It was always exciting when people stopped to buy pumpkins and handed me money. As the can filled, I carried it into the house and poured the contents into a pail that was almost full by Halloween.

Then one December day that was too cold for farming, Grandpa loaded me and my bucket of coins into the cab of his Ford pickup, and we went to the bank. With his help I lugged the bucket into the bank and up to a window where a kind teller waited for us. This was my introduction to banking. And so it went year after year: planting, cultivating, harvesting, selling and saving. Each year I took on a larger role in the pumpkin business. When I turned 16, I had enough pumpkin money to buy a candy apple red '57 Ford!

It's been many years since I last grew pumpkins, and Grandpa has been gone a long time. But his spirit and wisdom have been part of me since the day I first jumped on that hill of pumpkin seeds.

Jim, at age 7, heads to the fields to cultivate his pumpkins. In the patch, he learned about the value of hard work.

PUMPKIN CUTOUTS

PREP 30 min. + chilling **BAKE** 10 min./ batch + cooling **MAKES** about 3 dozen

- ½ cup shortening
- ¾ cup sugar
- ½ cup canned pumpkin pie mix
- ¼ cup molasses
- 3 cups all-purpose flour
- 1 tsp. baking soda
- 1 tsp. ground ginger
- 1 tsp. ground cinnamon
- ½ tsp. baking powder
- ½ tsp. salt

ICING

- 4 cups confectioners' sugar
- ⅓ cup butter, softened
- 3 to 4 Tbsp. 2% milk
- Food coloring, optional

1. Cream shortening and sugar until light and fluffy. Beat in pie mix and molasses. Whisk next 6 ingredients; gradually beat into creamed mixture. Divide dough in half; shape into 2 disks. Wrap separately; refrigerate several hours, until firm enough to roll.
2. Preheat the oven to 375°. On a lightly floured surface, roll each portion of dough to ¼-in. thickness. Cut with a floured 2½-in. pumpkin-shaped cookie cutter. Place cutouts 2 in. apart on greased baking sheets. Bake until the edges are firm, 8-10 minutes. Remove from pans to wire racks to cool completely.
3. For icing, beat confectioners' sugar, butter and enough milk to reach spreading consistency. If desired, tint with food coloring. Decorate as desired.

1 COOKIE 156 cal., 5g fat (2g sat. fat), 5mg chol., 94mg sod., 28g carb. (20g sugars, 0 fiber), 1g pro.

HARVEST APPLE CIDER

PREP 5 min. **COOK** 2 hours
MAKES about 2 qt.

- 8 whole cloves
- 4 cups apple cider or juice
- 4 cups pineapple juice
- ½ cup water
- 1 cinnamon stick (3 in.)
- 1 tea bag

1. Place cloves on a double thickness of cheesecloth; bring up corners of cloth and tie with kitchen string to form a bag. Place the remaining ingredients in a 3-qt. slow cooker.

2. Cover and cook on low until cider reaches desired temperature, about 2 hours. Discard spice bag, cinnamon stick and tea bag before serving.

1 CUP 130 cal., 0 fat (0 sat. fat), 0 chol., 14mg sod., 32g carb. (30g sugars, 0 fiber), 0 pro.

APPLE & HERB ROASTED TURKEY

PREP 20 min. **BAKE** 3 hours + standing
MAKES 14 servings

- ¼ cup minced fresh sage
- ¼ cup minced fresh rosemary
- 1 turkey (14 lbs.)
- 1 medium apple, quartered
- 1 medium onion, halved
- 1 celery rib, halved
- ½ cup butter, melted
- ½ cup apple jelly, warmed

1. Preheat oven to 325°. Combine sage and rosemary. With fingers, loosen skin from the turkey breast; rub herbs under the skin. Using toothpicks, secure skin to underside of breast.

2. Place breast side up on a rack in a roasting pan. Place apple, onion and celery in turkey cavity. Brush skin with butter.

3. Roast, uncovered, until a thermometer inserted in thickest part of thigh reads 170°-175°, 3-3½ hours. (Cover with foil if turkey browns too quickly.) Remove from oven; brush with jelly. Tent with foil and let stand 15 minutes before removing toothpicks and carving.

8 OZ. COOKED TURKEY 626 cal., 31g fat (11g sat. fat), 262mg chol., 222mg sod., 10g carb. (9g sugars, 0 fiber), 72g pro.

CINNAMON-PEAR RUSTIC TART

PREP 45 min. + chilling **BAKE** 45 min.
MAKES 8 servings

- 2½ cups all-purpose flour
- 1 tsp. salt
- 1 cup cold butter, cubed
- 8 to 10 Tbsp. ice water

FILLING

- 2 Tbsp. butter
- 8 medium ripe pears, peeled and thinly sliced
- 1½ tsp. ground cinnamon
- ⅓ cup apple cider or juice
- ¼ cup packed brown sugar
- 1 tsp. vanilla extract
- 1 Tbsp. coarse sugar

1. In a bowl, mix flour and salt; cut in butter until crumbly. Gradually add ice water, tossing with a fork until dough holds together when pressed. Shape dough into a disk; wrap.

Refrigerate for 30 minutes or overnight.

2. Preheat oven to 375°. In a large skillet, heat butter over medium-high heat. Add the pears and cinnamon; cook and stir until tender, 2-3 minutes. Stir in cider and brown sugar. Bring to a boil; stir until thickened, 8-10 minutes. Stir in vanilla; cool slightly.

3. On a lightly floured surface, roll dough into a 14-in. circle. Transfer to a parchment-lined baking sheet.

4. Spoon filling over crust to within 2 in. of edge. Fold crust edge over filling, pleating as you go and leaving an opening in the center. Brush folded crust with water; sprinkle with coarse sugar. Bake until the crust is golden and filling is bubbly, 45-50 minutes. Transfer tart to a wire rack to cool.

1 SLICE 512 cal., 27g fat (17g sat. fat), 69mg chol., 506mg sod., 67g carb. (27g sugars, 7g fiber), 5g pro.

MOM'S SWEET POTATO BAKE

PREP 10 min. **BAKE** 45 min.
MAKES 8 servings

- 3 cups cold mashed sweet potatoes (prepared without milk or butter)
- 1 cup sugar
- 3 large eggs
- ½ cup 2% milk
- ¼ cup butter, softened
- 1 tsp. salt
- 1 tsp. vanilla extract

TOPPING

- ½ cup packed brown sugar
- ½ cup chopped pecans
- ¼ cup all-purpose flour
- 2 Tbsp. cold butter

1. Preheat oven to 325°. In a large bowl, beat the sweet potatoes, sugar, eggs, milk, butter, salt and vanilla until smooth. Transfer to a greased 2-qt. baking dish.

2. In a small bowl, combine the brown sugar, pecans and flour; cut in butter until crumbly. Sprinkle over sweet potato mixture. Bake, uncovered, until a thermometer reads 160°, 45-50 minutes.

½ CUP 417 cal., 16g fat (7g sat. fat), 94mg chol., 435mg sod., 65g carb. (47g sugars, 4g fiber), 6g pro.

AUTUMN PUMPKIN CHILI

PREP 20 min. **COOK** 7 hours
MAKES 4 servings (1¼ qt.)

- 1 medium onion, chopped
- 1 small green pepper, chopped
- 1 small sweet yellow pepper, chopped
- 1 Tbsp. canola oil
- 1 garlic clove, minced
- 1 lb. ground turkey
- 1 can (15 oz.) solid-pack pumpkin
- 1 can (14½ oz.) diced tomatoes, undrained
- 4½ tsp. chili powder
- ¼ tsp. salt
- ¼ tsp. pepper
  Optional toppings: Shredded cheddar cheese, sour cream, corn chips and sliced green onions

1. In a large skillet, saute onion and the green and yellow peppers in oil until tender. Add garlic; cook 1 minute longer. Crumble turkey into skillet. Cook over medium heat until meat is no longer pink.

2. Transfer to a 3-qt. slow cooker. Stir in the pumpkin, tomatoes, chili powder, salt and pepper. Cover; cook on low for 7-9 hours. If desired, serve with cheese and other toppings.

1¼ CUPS 281 cal., 13g fat (3g sat. fat), 75mg chol., 468mg sod., 20g carb. (9g sugars, 7g fiber), 25g pro. **DIABETIC EXCHANGES** 3 lean meat, 1 starch, 1 vegetable, 1 fat

ACORN SQUASH WITH LEFTOVER STUFFING

PREP 20 min. **BAKE** 50 min.
MAKES 6 servings

- 3 small acorn squash
- 1 large egg, lightly beaten
- ¼ tsp. salt
- ⅛ tsp. pepper
- 1 tsp. chicken bouillon granules
- 2 Tbsp. boiling water
- 2 cups cooked stuffing
- ¼ cup grated Parmesan cheese, optional
- 1 tsp. paprika
  Chopped fresh parsley, optional

1. Cut squash in half; discard seeds. Place squash cut side down in a 15x10x1-in. baking pan; add ½ in. hot water. Bake, uncovered, at 400° until tender, about 30 minutes.

2. When squash is cool enough to handle, scoop out flesh, leaving a ¼-in. shell (flesh will measure about 3 cups). Drain water from pan; place squash shells cut side up in pan and set aside.

3. In a large bowl, combine the flesh, egg, salt and pepper. Dissolve bouillon in boiling water; add to squash mixture. Add stuffing; spoon into squash shells. If desired, top with cheese. Sprinkle with paprika. Bake, uncovered, at 400° until heated through, 20-25 minutes. If desired, sprinkle with chopped fresh parsley.

1 STUFFED SQUASH HALF 240 cal., 8g fat (2g sat. fat), 38mg chol., 680mg sod., 39g carb. (7g sugars, 5g fiber), 6g pro.

SIMPLE CHICKEN ENCHILADAS

PREP 20 min. **BAKE** 25 min.
MAKES 5 servings

- 1 can (10 oz.) enchilada sauce, divided
- 4 oz. cream cheese, cubed
- 1½ cups salsa
- 2 cups cubed cooked chicken
- 1 can (15 oz.) pinto beans, rinsed and drained
- 1 can (4 oz.) chopped green chiles
- 10 flour tortillas (6 in.)
- 1 cup shredded Mexican cheese blend
- Optional: Shredded lettuce, chopped tomato, sour cream and sliced ripe olives

1. Preheat oven to 350°. Spoon ½ cup enchilada sauce into a greased 13x9-in. baking dish. In a saucepan, cook and stir cream cheese and salsa over medium heat until blended, 2-3 minutes. Stir in the chicken, beans and chiles.

2. Place about ⅓ cup chicken mixture down the center of each tortilla. Roll up; place seam side down over sauce. Top with remaining sauce; sprinkle with shredded cheese.

3. Cover and bake until heated through, 25-30 minutes. If desired, serve with toppings.

2 ENCHILADAS 468 cal., 13g fat (6g sat. fat), 75mg chol., 1394mg sod., 51g carb. (6g sugars, 8g fiber), 34g pro.

SKILLET SHEPHERD'S PIE

TAKES 30 min. **MAKES** 6 servings

- 1 lb. ground beef
- 1 cup chopped onion
- 2 cups frozen corn, thawed
- 2 cups frozen peas, thawed
- 2 Tbsp. ketchup
- 1 Tbsp. Worcestershire sauce
- 2 tsp. minced garlic
- 1 Tbsp. cornstarch
- 1 tsp. beef bouillon granules
- ½ cup cold water
- ½ cup sour cream
- 3½ cups mashed potatoes (prepared with milk and butter)
- ¾ cup shredded cheddar cheese

1. In a skillet, cook beef and onion over medium heat until meat is no longer pink; drain. Stir in the corn, peas, ketchup, Worcestershire sauce and garlic. Reduce heat to medium-low; cover and cook for 5 minutes.

2. Combine cornstarch, bouillon and water until well blended; stir into beef mixture. Bring to a boil over medium heat; cook and stir until thickened, 2 minutes. Stir in sour cream and heat through (do not boil).

3. Spread mashed potatoes over the top; sprinkle with cheese. Cover and cook until the potatoes are heated through and cheese is fully melted.

1 SERVING 448 cal., 20g fat (12g sat. fat), 80mg chol., 781mg sod., 45g carb. (8g sugars, 7g fiber), 24g pro.

Handcrafted

CREATE A FEELING OF HOME

CRAFT YOUR THANKS

WHAT YOU'LL NEED

Small screws
Open frame
Twine
Wood
Scrapbook paper
Decorative tacks
Scrabble letters
Paper leaves
Mini clothespins
Hot glue gun

DIRECTIONS

1. Attach small screw eyes on back of an open frame along both vertical sides, roughly 2 in. apart.
2. Tie a knot in a length of twine and thread through an eye at bottom of frame.
3. Weave the twine back and forth through the eyes, working up and then back down, crossing twine from side to side. Pull the twine tightly and knot on last eye.
4. Cut a piece of wood to fit the frame's bottom corner, and trim a piece of scrapbook paper slightly smaller than wood. Hot-glue paper to wood. Layer wooden craft leaves along sides and hot-glue into place.
5. Press decorative tacks into corners of scrapbook paper.
6. Using old Scrabble letters, spell out a message on board. Hot-glue letters into place. Hot-glue wood piece onto frame. Add any additional embellishments as desired.
7. Add paper leaves to frame with mini clothespins.

GOLDEN GRATITUDE

WHAT YOU'LL NEED
Pumpkin
Cream and gold acrylic craft paint
Chalk
Paintbrushes
Hot glue gun
Rags

DIRECTIONS
1. Using a wide brush, paint pumpkin with cream paint.
2. Write "thankful" on pumpkin with chalk. Trace over lettering with hot glue. Dry thoroughly.
3. Paint 2-3 coats of gold paint over letters with small brush.
4. Using a large brush, apply thin coat of gold paint over pumpkin, increasing concentration of paint in creases. Remove any excess paint with a rag, using small circular motions. Paint stem gold. Dry thoroughly.
5. Paint a thin coat of cream paint over pumpkin's ridges, removing excess with a rag. Dry thoroughly.

HELLO, SUNSHINE

WHAT YOU'LL NEED
Assorted greens (lemon, olive and bay leaves, rosemary, and seeded eucalyptus work well)
Covered binding wire
24-in. round wire wreath frame
Toothpick
10-14 assorted oranges, lemons, clementines and kumquats
Whole cloves
20-gauge wire
Wire cutters

DIRECTIONS
1. Trim greens into 8- to 12-in. lengths. Using binding wire, bind together 12-15 small bundles of greenery, leaving wire tails to secure each bundle to frame.
2. Position bundles on frame, overlapping slightly. Using wire tails, secure to frame; trim ends.
3. Using toothpick, poke pattern of holes into 1 side of several pieces of fruit and insert whole cloves. Thread a piece of 20-gauge wire through oranges, lemons and clementines and attach to wreath as desired. Trim ends. (Avoid twisting wire too tightly, or it will slice through the fruit.)
4. Make kumquat bundles by threading a piece of 20-gauge wire through 2 kumquats. Gently bend wire ends down and twist together below the kumquats. Attach bundles to frame. Trim the ends.

Winter

Snow blankets the landscape around
the Tully River in Massachusetts
just before dawn, creating
a breathtaking woodland scene.

The Good Life

APPRECIATE THE SIMPLE PLEASURES

WHEN MOOSE COME CALLING

At our fly-in lodge in Alaska, every day is an adventure.

BONNIE BRAMANTE TALKEETNA MOUNTAINS, ALASKA

I always smile when people ask me where I live. My response, "15 air miles from Talkeetna," is followed by a parade of questions. Only in Alaska is this an acceptable address.

Five years ago, my husband, Joe, and I left our small-town life and moved to the remote wilderness of central Alaska. No neighbors (except an occasional moose), no roads and no outside power—complete immersion into off-grid living.

The two of us partnered with Joe's brother, Zac, and his wife, Alyssa, in owning and operating Caribou Lodge, a fly-in lodge situated at the edge of an alpine lake in the pretty foothills of the

Talkeetna Mountains (closer to Denali than the national park's headquarters is). Little did any of us know the adventures we'd have as we attempted to carve out a life in the middle of untouched wilderness. Unlike most lodge owners in Alaska, we live here year-round (with our baby girl, Emma), and each season has its own unique challenges.

Summer is a whirlwind, with guests coming from all over the world to hike and explore. Our operation is small and family-run, with three cozy cabins plus the main lodge, where everyone gathers to dine on hearty, home-cooked meals or sip coffee out on the deck with our lovable dog, Howie, at their feet. Floatplanes skim across the lake, bringing supplies and day hikers. Days are long, with the sun setting around midnight and barely dipping below the peaks before it rises again.

I love the early-morning hours when I get up to clean. The guests are fast asleep, and wisps of fog lift off the lake as the

Bonnie answers the door expecting company, not a moose (far left). But that is just a part of life at Caribou Lodge (top), where floatplanes occupy the "parking lot."

sunshine shimmers across it. The loon's call is haunting in the silence.

By the end of August, blueberries are ripe and everyone's harvesting. Guests return from hikes with water bottles filled with berries. Zac and Alyssa's girls are always looking for one of us to take them out to pick blueberries. Chloe, 6, fills her bucket quickly and as efficiently as most adults. Eiley, 4, barely covers the bottom of her bucket because most of her berries end up in Howie's and her mouths. Zac and Joe clean berries in the evenings while Alyssa and I spend any free time canning as much blueberry jelly as possible. Harvesting food from the land to fill our pantry for the long winter is so rewarding.

Fall is my favorite time of year. The tundra is a gorgeous blaze of red and gold, and bears can be spotted meandering the hillsides, filling up on berries to prepare for a season of hibernation. It also signals the return of nightfall, when the northern lights dance and stars shine unobscured by city lights.

Trumpeter swans, as well as sandhill cranes, stop by during migration. The

" Snow teases us through October and November and is here to stay by December."

In the winter, riding snow machines in the foothills (above) is a favorite pastime for the Bramante family (top left). On this trip, Howie and his dog buddy Ike came along (top right), taking turns riding in and running beside the sled.

swans are serene and graceful, while the cranes are all wings and noise.

As the fall colors ebb and we wake up to morning frost, the summer tourist season ends and we get the place to ourselves. We hike slowly with children and dogs in tow, soaking up sunshine, and begin preparing for winter. By the first week of October, we get our last supply flight before freeze-up. We wave goodbye to the pilot, knowing that our time of solitude has begun. No planes fly in or out during the freeze-up; an expensive helicopter ride is the only way in or out by air. So, for two months we hunker down and watch the days grow shorter. Snow teases us in October and November and stays by December.

When I lived in town, I tolerated the Alaskan winters, but here I love them. We get out snowmobiles—or snow machines, as Alaskans call them—and head out for supplies. Once the marshes and river freeze and the snow falls, we can access a trail to a trailhead outside Talkeetna, where we park our truck at the end of summer. It's about an hourlong ride there, with breathtaking views of Denali along the way. We use the trail to haul our supplies in and out all winter, and friends follow it to the lodge for the weekend. Joe grooms a nice long cross-country ski track, along with a sledding run down Blueberry Hill.

While we do a lot of shoveling and packing trails, winter is our rest time. On stormy days we curl up by the fire with a big cup of hot cocoa or coffee and get lost in a book, or head up to the lodge for an extremely competitive board game with Zac and Alyssa. As I write, it's the end of May. Rain pours outside my window. The landscape is wrapped in shades of gray, and a pair of goldeneye ducks swim along the edge of the lake where the ice has retreated from the shore. Patches of snow cling to the hillsides above the muted brown tones of the tundra.

In town, our friends mow green grass and plant flowers, but up here, spring comes slowly, almost painfully so. The years have been a long lesson in waiting, watching and bending to nature's rhythm. Just outside our door, we witness wildlife in their natural habitat, living our daily lives alongside them and becoming as changeable as the seasons around us.

Winter here is gorgeous (top), but sometimes a little holiday decorating brightens the landscape. For their first Christmas at the lodge, Joe decorated the bear cache with lights powered by a generator.

'WE'LL FIX IT TOGETHER'

Fifty years ago, the rickety family farmhouse became home sweet home.

MARJI STEVENS HONEOYE FALLS, NEW YORK

A canopy of trees arched over the quaintest country road I'd ever seen. The sign read Stoney Lonesome Road, a hidden gem just south of Rochester, New York. Soon we eased out onto an open road where barns garnished rolling hills, and golden wheat fields stretched out before us like giant patches in a homemade quilt.

We pulled onto a dirt driveway that led to the top of a high ridge.

"You can see the entire property from up here," said my fiance, Bill. "My grandparents grew the best strawberries and cantaloupe in Monroe County. People came for miles." His words trailed off as if the view had carried him to a different time. "I love it here."

I wasn't a "country" girl, but the land took my breath away. Far in the distance,

I saw Bristol Mountain, known by many for its 1,200-foot vertical rise, skirted with rolling hills. The farm is located in the one-traffic-light town of Rush.

"This is the perfect location," Bill said. "It's 20 minutes south of Rochester and 20 minutes north of the Finger Lakes."

We jostled back down the drive and onto Rush Mendon Road until we arrived at a small farmhouse with peeling paint and forest green gingerbread trim. "This is it!" Bill said, rolling down his window. "This is where we're going to live someday."

The house that had belonged to his grandparents had been vacant for many years—and it was in serious disrepair. There were no closets, locks or insulation, and the bathroom floor slanted south.

A huge horse chestnut tree in bloom shaded the front yard. Tall blue spruce

trees circled the house like a giant castle wall and backed up to 70 acres of fertile farmland. Peonies peeked from among the spirea bushes all along the narrow gravel driveway, and a gray hay barn stood about 50 yards behind the house.

"What's that sound?" I asked.

"Bees—probably hundreds of them. Two to a bloom, I imagine. Can't you see us living here?"

The house part concerned me, but I could see myself painting the view from the top of that ridge. This place had a lot of potential.

"See that great side porch?" Bill asked. "I want to spend the rest of my life sitting there with you." He squeezed my shoulder. "As soon as I'm out of the military, we'll move back home and sit on that porch. We'll fix it together."

The Vietnam War was at its peak. Tears came to my eyes as I thought about him leaving. "As long as we're together, I'll be happy," I said.

Four years later, Bill was discharged from the Army, and we moved into the farmhouse as he promised.

This somewhat spoiled suburban girl followed the love of her life and became a country girl as our family grew to include two sons, Kyle and Jonathan.

Over time we added a couple of scruffy barn cats and an oversized rescue dog, chickens and a huge organic garden. The repairs to the weathered farmhouse made

it uniquely ours, and lovely, but my favorite part remains the land. A section of the Lehigh Valley Railroad used to go through the center of the farm. Bill's dad hopped that train to get to school. It's since been replaced with a walking and biking trail that stretches for miles.

Winters here can be long and gray, but they afford the creative soul many quiet hours to paint and write. Precious winter memories remain of snow-covered mittens drying by the front door, a fire crackling in the wood stove, ice-tipped branches tapping against my window, and the warmth of a happy home.

The cold days are sandwiched between splendid springs, with the Lilac Festival at Highland Park, and the unmatched beauty of the Finger Lakes in fall, when the hillsides are ablaze with colors.

I find it hard to imagine that 50 years have passed since I first moved to this house. Now I am a widow. My sons live close by, and seven grandchildren play in the fields. Five generations of Stevenses have crossed the threshold of this home. The old chestnut tree has come down now, but new trees flourish in the yard, and the same peonies that Bill's grandmother planted grace the walkway.

The old side porch where our dreams began is still my favorite place to be, as I consider how fortunate I am to live surrounded by a rich history, family, beautiful country and so many blessings.

Marji's husband, Bill, dreamed of raising their children on the old farm. Now grandkids have the run of the place, racing past the peonies.

Mandi and Brandon (opposite top left) chose to raise their children on land in the north Georgia mountains (above).

HOME ON THE MOUNTAIN

Dandelions and fishing poles replace cellphones and TV remotes
in our neck of the Georgia woods.

MANDI WOOD EASTANOLLEE, GEORGIA

Brandon, my sweet husband, always tells me, "Home is where you lay your head." It's a sanctuary where you live your best life with family...when you're not scrubbing a stack of dishes, washing ever-growing piles of laundry and blowing dust bunnies out of every corner.

Though Brandon and I are both from Georgia, we come from very different parts of the state. Brandon grew up in southern Georgia's Okefenokee Swamp. Alligators and bugs galore! He likes to tell the story about the day his ball splashed into the Altamaha River. Brandon waded into the muddy waters to retrieve it and saw a log floating by. His daddy yelled at

him to stay still until the log drifted farther down the river. Back safely on the riverbank, Brandon learned that the log was actually a gator. On the other hand, I spent my childhood in northeastern Georgia, where my daddy taught me to love the Blue Ridge Mountains.

I remember exploring the back roads with my parents. Brasstown Bald, the state's highest peak, was a favorite of ours. Mine was a perfect childhood—a gift that I knew I'd pass on to my own kids.

So when Brandon and I married, we chose to make our home near Currahee Mountain in northern Georgia. Our children—Addie, 19; Connor, 14; Colston, 12; Christian, 6; and Nava Grace, 1—have

the freedom to roam. Life on the mountain is good in all four seasons of the year.

Our house sits atop a hill overlooking a quiet oval pond covered in lily pads, and it is surrounded by lush farmlands and a bounty of wildlife. The pond isn't so quiet as summer approaches, though. The sound of bullfrogs singing (a sure sign of summer) is a bit deafening.

The boys love to fish and play at the water's edge. Our dog, Ford, is a true water dog. Lovingly named for Brandon's truck, Ford jumps in the pond and swims as the boys fish.

It gets so hot and humid here in the summer that setting out the sprinkler is a fun way to find relief. When the evening sky turns all shades of pink and cotton-candy colors, we throw a blanket in the driveway and take turns pointing out the different cloud formations and describing what shapes we see. We finish the night out on the porch, sitting under strands of twinkling lights and drinking sweet tea in glass jars.

As the winds blow harder and the air grows colder in fall, the kids and I finish our home-school work at our beautiful old kitchen table. After the books are shut and the pencils are put away, we make cups of rich hot chocolate topped with a hearty dollop of fresh whipped cream. Then we sit on the front porch, which overlooks the long grassy fields and farm fences, and I snuggle with the littlest ones on the swing with blankets.

In the mountains, autumn is a show. When the kids play in the front yard, they run as fast as they can to catch falling leaves before they land on the ground.

Christian dips his toes on a warm summer day (top). Nava Grace listens intently during a church service; Ford, the feisty family dog, takes a break after playing with the boys.

At night, we listen to the wild coyotes yip and howl. I can tell you it's excitingly eerie and neat to hear the pack howling together in the deep woods across the road. Connor has a coyote yip imitation down pat and can get them started up at night. He wants to work with wildlife one day.

Winters can be unpredictable.

As any good Southerner knows, you could be tanning in the hot sun one day and building a snowman the next. We rarely have a white Christmas, so when we see flakes falling from the sky and fluttering in the air, we get super excited. The farther north you roam into the mountains, the more snow you will see. Brasstown Bald is covered in snow and ice most of the winter.

No matter the season, nature just runs through our blood. We hold dandelions and fishing poles instead of cellphones and remotes. As long as we have each other, we are already home. And home, my friends, is a beautiful thing.

> **As long as we have each other, we are already home."**

The woods and waters surrounding Mandi's home give her children hours of exploration (top). When snow falls, Christian ventures out to enjoy himself in the winter playground.

A MAN FOR ALL SEASONS

No fickle love here. Wisconsin has my heart in spite of the rain, humidity, mosquitoes and snow.

CHAD WESTON GARDNER OMRO, WISCONSIN

Seems to me there are many people mocking Wisconsinites for living in the Dairy State, particularly when it's cold here and warm where they are. Fair enough, I'll bite. Here's why I choose to live in Wisconsin...

The truth is, I'm in love with the four seasons. And not just a flash-in-the-pan love. I mean a lifelong love—for better or for worse, in snowstorms and in humidity, until drought do us part.

I love the hope that spring in Wisconsin delivers, when we can watch the world come alive once again. The icy grip of cold weather is fractured, and the new season's sunny sneak previews shine through. They are coming attractions of cherished memories not yet created and shared.

I love the warmth of summer, when the sun's heat is only slightly hotter than the warmth of all of us gathered together. I'm thankful for unplanned summer days that end in sunsets that resemble a picture of a beautiful soul.

I love a crisp Wisconsin fall. The world becomes a vibrant canvas of embers—the trees glowing as if in a chorus of flames, and all the world has a front-row seat. As the heat gives way to cool nights, an open window on a mid-October night turns sleep into slumber.

I love the incredible beauty of winter, when the world rests in soft hibernation beneath a blanket of snow. The outside world nudges us inside, to cuddle under afghans and snuggle close to the warmest of hearts. It's a beautiful retreat into our own private cocoons.

So, you can have your warm year-round weather all to yourself. To me, that kind of climate is like those flashy characters at a party who have no depth. Once their flashiness grows old, there isn't much more interesting about them.

I'll stick with the one that keeps me alive, makes me feel and shows me all sides of life. Yes, I'll gladly grow old with that one.

Scenes like this one at Racine's Wind Point Lighthouse help Chad embrace Wisconsin's icy weather.

Scrapbook

1

2

1. A PERFECT PAL

Whether going on a wild hen chase or making the most of each season, our farm dog, Remi, is a golden bundle of fun.

MEGAN MEYER SABETHA, KANSAS

2. FOLLOW THE LEADER

My husband and I had to go after some new heifer calves who'd gone astray. In sunshine or snow, this is our little slice of heaven.

AMBER ANDERSON COTTONWOOD, IDAHO

2

3

1. THE GATHERING PLACE

This is Miners' Park in Windber, Pennsylvania, and it's a focal point for this small town at Christmastime.

CAROL SAYLOR MEYERSDALE, PENNSYLVANIA

2. PERFECT TREAT

My children—Audrey, 6, Seth, 10, and Lucas, 8—warm up with hot cocoa after sledding on our farm.

ANDREA BURNS DENTON, MARYLAND

3. A SPECTACULAR SIGHT

A recent winter brought a rare influx of snowy owls. We heard that one snowy was consistently seen at a local farm, so we headed there, hoping to catch a glimpse. When we arrived, this majestic bird seemed to be calmly waiting for us. We shared the same space for about 10 minutes before it moved on. It was a beautiful moment despite the subzero temperature. Winter is glorious here.

KATIE HEADE MASSILLON, OHIO

1. PRECIOUS CARGO

My husband, Ryan, gives our grandson Rynn a special sled ride during a Christmastime visit.

COLLEEN GAUSMAN THORP, WASHINGTON

2. GUARD DOGS

Moxie and Sunny make sure to keep a keen eye on our farm pond.

LISA CARE FLEETWOOD, PENNSYLVANIA

3. PRETTY AS A PICTURE

My granddaughter Lilly and I did a little photo shoot in our barn. She was very cooperative, and we enjoyed spending this time together as she modeled for me among the decorations.

CAROL SAYLOR MEYERSDALE, PENNSYLVANIA

3

FROZEN BEAUTY

Fantastic shades of blue in Rock Creek in Montana's Beartooth Mountains are the result of "anchor ice" or "ice gorging." Free-floating ice crystals collect at the bottom of the fast-moving stream.

RENEE LUND RED LODGE, MONTANA

1. ICY BEAUTY

While exploring ice caves at Apostle Islands National Lakeshore along Lake Superior in Wisconsin, I could see a dramatic contrast between the rock outcroppings where trees grow upside down and the ice formations below that are as unique as snowflakes.

LISA MESHESKI WAUKESHA, WISCONSIN

2. HAPPY HOLIDAYS

The magic of snow brought my daughter and her new stepbrother outside. It was our first holiday season as a family.

JESS TAYLOR GREENSBORO, NORTH CAROLINA

3. MERRY AND BRIGHT LIGHTS

Christmas is my favorite time of year. I decorate our little country home with lights, wreaths and red bows. The snow added an extra touch.

SHARON CAMPBELL RUCKERSVILLE, VIRGINIA

1. JUST LIKE REAL LIFE

My daughter Rebekah (left), my sister Jenn (second from left), my daughter Abigail (right) and I made gingerbread renditions of my Cape Cod home. Notice the addition of Rebekah's bunny hutch.

ANNE DUVALL GREENCASTLE, PENNSYLVANIA

2. DAZZLING DISPLAY

Our family Christmas tradition is viewing the 4 million lights along the Mississippi River in La Crosse, Wisconsin. And we love the hot cocoa, carriage rides, s'mores and visits with Santa Claus!

LINDA ZIEGLER WESTBY, WISCONSIN

3. ON DASHER, ON DANCER!

We moved to Alaska, where we visited a reindeer ranch. I can't think of a better Christmas experience than walking with a reindeer along a snowy trail.

KATHY CROSS SOLDOTNA, ALASKA

1. A POP OF COLOR

One of the joys of cold winter days is filling the bird feeder and watching—from inside my home—the comings and goings of feathered friends like this house finch.

DEBBIE BIDDLE SENECA, SOUTH CAROLINA

2. FARMALL FESTIVE

My husband and I made this wreath for our 1953 Super C. We have chickens and grow vegetables, and he also raises beef cattle, corn and soybeans with his dad, uncle and grandpa.

KELLI LAGE SHEFFIELD, IOWA

3. HOLIDAY SWEETNESS

My stepdaughter Nicole gives adorable sled dog Ryobi a little kiss under the holiday mistletoe.

LEA FRYE NATHROP, COLORADO

1. TINY TREASURES
Christmas is the time to share smiles, and this fun and happy photo of our family pets seems to do the job.

MITCHELL McCLOSKY BREWSTER, WASHINGTON

2. FAMILY FIREWOOD
My husband, Jason, and our son Ethan bundled up to collect firewood so we didn't have to bundle up in the house during the cold winter months!

JERIANN TRUITT DAGGETT, MICHIGAN

3. THE SPIRIT OF THE SEASON
I love this photo because it shows the first year our oldest really seemed to grasp the excitement of the Christmas season. He was jumping all around the living room, excited to put up every decoration and hang every ornament on the tree. It is such a treasure to watch a child and their joy around Christmas! It will forever be a special memory for me.

AMY SMITH HILLSBORO, KANSAS

Heart & Soul

A CHRISTMAS TREE QUEST

Special holiday memories inspired an adventurous outing that
I hope my sons will remember forever.

GARY HOUK LEAGUE CITY, TEXAS

I was an Air Force brat for my first 12 years. The transient military lifestyle didn't offer memorable Christmases: the tiny two-bedroom house of a widowed aunt in Blytheville, Arkansas; a cramped motel room in Omaha, Nebraska; bland cookie-cutter duplexes in base housing. But within those 12 years fell 1967. I was 9 years old.

With Dad deployed to Vietnam. Mom and we four kids settled in the tiny cotton town of Madison, Alabama, for the length of Dad's absence. Madison was close to the cradle of their childhoods: Paint Rock Valley, a 30-mile stretch of Cumberland Plateau populated by corn and soybean fields, deep coves, limestone caves, and more relatives than mice in a barn.

Grandma and Grandpa lived at the end of a long dirt lane that crossed Lick Fork Creek, ran smooth through bottomland, and finished bumpy near the base of Putman Mountain. Until 1967, we had

visited the valley only a few times. Though we barely knew our grandparents or the farm, we loved them very much.

Christmas 1967 found us tucked away, deep in the narrow cove that protected the homestead. Lying in bed the first night of our visit, I wondered, *Would Santa find us?* Up until then he had tracked us down all over the world.

I pulled the warm bedclothes over my shoulders and all the way to my chin. Glowing embers in a potbellied stove set me adrift in an ocean of Grandma's heavy quilts. Tomorrow the men would search for a Christmas tree.

The odd-shaped and scrawny pines in our nearby woods posed little threat to the symmetrically trimmed perfection of their city cousins, but the fun was in the finding. My brother Randy and I set out with Grandpa—he with a sharp ax, we with sharp eyes. It's a romantic notion to think nature's hands would never create an ugly evergreen. But our eyes knew what ugly looked like; on this day it was spread all over the place in the form of lumpy little pines. We scouted for a couple of hours before settling on the pine tree equivalent of a sad-faced clown.

We begged and pleaded, but Grandpa wouldn't let us swing the ax. "Save your energy to haul the tree home," he told us as Randy and I watched him fell our quarry. We got it to the house and, after piling on layer upon layer of tinsel, bulbs and lights, we transformed our little pine into the envy of Times Square and the White House.

I'm now a husband and father. Normally I relive the Christmas of 1967 in my mind, but one year I convinced my wife to trade city-bought evergreen boughs for the twisted branches of wild pine.

I bundled up our two boys, Kyle and Ryan, in warm layers and hunter orange caps. We grabbed snacks and a hatchet, and drove to my grandparents' farm. They had retired and moved closer to city conveniences. One of my cousins now worked the farm, but the old house stood empty of everything but good memories.

I pulled off the muddy lane and we stepped outside into the cold. Words turned into little clouds as they rolled out of our mouths. At ages 7 and 8, the boys weren't quite as into the adventure as I had been at 9. *They're also too young to recognize ugly,* I thought.

We scouted fence rows and overgrown pastures for a while. The boys found many trees to their liking, but I held fast to the notion of a perfect Christmas tree. I was creating a memory that I hoped would last.

I've never asked my sons if they recall our chilly tree excursion, or the rather nondescript little specimen we hauled home, or that they had chopped it down. I do hope they bring it up someday, for my memory of searching for a special tree more than 50 years ago settles snugly around me like thick, warm quilts on a cold night. I wish the same for them.

Sons Kyle and Ryan (above and top) searched for the perfect pine at Gary's grandparents' homestead in Alabama, which offered more adventure than an everyday tree farm.

DO YOU SEE WHAT I SEE?

In the hustle and bustle of the holidays, I discovered that my girls understood the real reason for the season.

MARILYN HOUGHTON KAYTON NAPERVILLE, ILLINOIS

One holiday season in the 1970s, my husband, Chuck, handled all the outside lights and I took care of all of the interior decorations. In addition, I had to bake the cutout cookies, make chocolate truffles, shampoo the carpeting, address holiday cards, organize church activities, wrap presents, polish the silver, plan an open house, shop for a turkey, write a story for the Christmas Eve service...the list went on. On top of all that, I was fighting a scratchy throat and a dull headache.

I finished dusting, vacuuming and decorating the living room. It looked splendid with a tree full of ornaments in designer colors, vanilla-scented candles, and our Italian Nativity scene on the coffee table, accented with pine boughs and a china dish containing frankincense. I was proud of the authentic touch.

"Well," I said proudly as I stood back to view the room, "at least one room is ready for company."

I ran into the kitchen to check the oven for burning cookies, then I addressed a few cards and ran to hand Chuck the outdoor lights. As I passed the living room, I noticed that the three wise men and camels were now on the piano and that the tiny manger was empty.

"Girls, get in here immediately!" Nina and Nancy came running.

"Who has been messing with my Nativity scene?" I asked. "I don't think you girls have any idea how hard I work to make a nice house for you. When I decorate, I expect things to stay in place. Who moved the three wise men?"

Nina, age 7, replied, "Mother, you don't understand. The wise men haven't arrived yet. They shouldn't be in the stable so we put them on the piano with the camels. And Baby Jesus hasn't been born, so we put him in the desk drawer."

"We'll put him out on Christmas Eve," said Nancy, hands on her hips. I was stunned. They had been listening to the story and showed a real feeling for the details. The wise men shouldn't be at the stable yet, and the Baby Jesus wouldn't be born until Christmas Eve.

I gave the girls a big hug and said, "You really did hear the story. We'll put Baby Jesus in the manger after we get home from Christmas Eve service. When should we move the wise men and camels over to the coffee table?"

I was decorating a living room; they were living the story.

Nancy and Nina share in a favorite holiday tradition—the yearly visit to Santa to discuss their wish lists.

Joseph (far right) and his family pose for a photo in front of the house they nearly lost.

OUR BEST CHRISTMAS

The fire that threatened our home over the holidays ended up strengthening our family and showing us what matters.

JOSEPH HAMRICK COMMERCE, TEXAS

Mom stood in silence. Her sister held her and reassured her as they watched the scene unfold through my aunt's kitchen window. Across the street, fire burned and smoke billowed from our home that Christmas Eve in 2007. The utter sadness on Mom's face will forever be etched in my memory.

Hours earlier, guests had arrived and both houses were full. We totaled 25, including my cousin Shonna and her husband, Bob, who both had just returned from serving in Iraq, and a few pets. My parents hosted half the guests. It was a veritable hostel.

It was chilly that night, and Dad stuffed the fireplace with more wood than usual. Firefighters later revealed that the builder had taken shortcuts on it: Cracks and holes gaped between the bricks, so a large fire burning long enough could spread.

After midnight, a smoke detector went off. Mom was the first to hear it. When she realized the house was on fire, she banged on doors to wake everyone up. We tried to save as much as we could. Dad removed important documents and family pictures off the wall. My sister Joanna grabbed her dog. Jamie, my oldest sister, snatched the stockings, which she said were essentials.

After waking everyone, Mom bolted across the street to rouse my aunt and uncle, who woke others in their house.

Every able person there ran to our house to salvage what they could. My cousin and his brother-in-law heaved my mother's great-great-grandmother's quilt cabinet from the house and onto the lawn.

After the police and firefighters arrived, we went from a frenzied rush to standing by helplessly and watching as the first responders tried to save the house where we had planned to open presents on Christmas morning. Furniture, pictures, electronics and keepsakes were strewn across the yard, but we all escaped alive.

In the end, firefighters saved the house, but it wasn't safe to go back in. All 25 of us crammed into Aunt Kim's. We didn't sleep. After the adrenaline wore off, many tears were shed. But morning arrived with a strange peace; it was hard not to be happy on Christmas. We opened what gifts we had, ate breakfast and spent time together.

The next day I was supposed to return to work, but I called in. I hadn't seen my parents or other family for a while, and the harrowing night made me realize I had been neglecting them.

We recently reminisced about the fire and the good that came from it. The house was rebuilt, the pictures rehung and the quilt cabinet returned to its place. We lost things, but our family now appreciates what matters. That was one of our best Christmases ever.

The peace of this church in Chautauqua County offered Judy a moment of quiet contemplation and inspiration.

SACRED SPACES

Find silent moments of soothing beauty and inner peace in places that invite you to stop, enter and listen.

JUDY WRODA ASHVILLE, NEW YORK

There are many quiet country roads here in Chautauqua County, New York—some are quieter than others, some made of dirt and rock, others of pavement and industry. I love exploring these roads, letting my soul search out the depths of their history and the serenity of God's beautiful creation.

A former church from the early 1800s stands on one of these roads. It's filled with stories of the beginnings of this area, forever entwined in the history of nearby families who made it their spiritual home.

One day as I was out walking, I found myself in front of this old church. It was a gray day of too much thinking and not enough "seeing." I stopped and looked up from the road, gazing upon this sturdy building through the frozen brush. I was cold, alone and wanted someone to talk to.

For a moment, my mind quieted. I had no racing thoughts and no direction to my feet. I had wandered, finding my way to this refuge of comfort and warmth on a bitter day of cold, blustery winds.

The song "Church in the Wildwood" bubbled from my heart, and I hummed the melody as I gazed upon this antiquated structure. I could feel the frigid air cutting through my heavy coat, and my fingers shook as I raised my camera. But through this shaking from deep emotions and winter's chill, I looked up to Heaven, said a quiet "thank you," and took this serene photo, my favorite of the day.

I took many more photos of the old church, but this first one captured what my soul was feeling: acceptance in the turmoil and indecision of life. I felt at peace and calmer, and my heart was happily humming "Just as I Am."

Listening intently to the song as it drifted upon the brittle winds, I heard it mingle with the melodies of the brave little birds fluttering about the fields and brush. I took a deep breath, let it out slowly and hushed my song for a bit so that I could listen to the stillness of nature around me—to hear what I was meant to hear. I let my thoughts flow; whether they were jumbled or made sense was of no matter. I knew God was listening, nonjudgmental and patient. I needed that time; we all need "that time." I found it here, at this old church, standing resolute against the backdrop of a forgotten era.

As I walked away from my scene of inspiration, I found myself hoping that all of you are able to find that place, that time where you can rest for a moment and just breathe. When you find it, close your eyes for a moment, walk to the double doors, push down on the latch and walk in. There is always someone there waiting to listen.

GUARDIAN ANGEL

A gentle dog and the wonders of pet therapy bring joy to children
and patients alike.

JILL BERNICK CAMARILLO, CALIFORNIA

Twenty years ago I became involved in pet therapy work. After our first golden retriever, J.J., passed away, we got another golden retriever puppy, whom we named J.J.'s Angel. As she matured and went through obedience training, we realized that she, too, would be a good therapy dog.

Angel is 10 now and works every week. She visits two hospitals, a day care for the elderly, and our library for the PAWS for Reading program. At the library, six to 10 dogs lie on the floor and the kids pick a book to read to a dog. After they finish, they get a trading card with the dog's picture and history.

Our sweet Angel has also helped out at a children's special-needs church camp. She is so popular that everywhere we go people recognize her, especially the kids who have read to her.

We have seen some special things happen through our pet therapy work.

I brought Angel to our local hospital to visit a woman who was fully paralyzed on her right side from a stroke. We spent time with her every week. Once my husband, Jack, got Angel up into a chair next to the woman's bed. He asked her if she wanted to give Angel a treat. She nodded yes, and Jack carefully placed the treat in the woman's right hand.

Angel gently took the treat out of her hand. Then the woman raised her right hand and she started petting Angel. Her friend was in the room and said, "She hasn't been able to move that hand since she had her stroke!" After that, every time we saw the woman she lifted her left hand. We told her she had to use her right hand, and she did.

When Angel visits the hospital she also performs tricks for the patients. We taught her how to say a prayer. She crouches on the floor, bows her head and crosses her paws. She stays very still and doesn't move until Jack says "Amen" and claps his hands.

Our 15-year-old grandson, David, helps us at the hospital to earn volunteer credits when he's not in school. After visiting, he says, "It's so neat to see how happy Angel makes the patients." And I say, "That's why we do it."

Angel bows her head and prays until Jill's husband, Jack, says "Amen" and claps his hands.

STITCHING TOGETHER MEMORIES

Grandmother's skills left a legacy of handiwork that is treasured
by everyone in the family.

BEVERLY SCHULTZ AURORA, COLORADO

The best thing about visiting Grandmother was exploring her sewing room. It was piled to the ceiling with more fabric, thread, zippers and pieces of half-finished garments than I had ever seen. A full-time working tailor, she made dresses, suits, wedding dresses, bathing suits and even drapes.

But when Grandmother visited us, it was even more fun, because I knew that she was going to sew for me! She sewed lickety-split as I sat watching her, and delighted me by telling funny stories of my mother when she was a little girl. Then she'd present me with a new dress, or frock, as she called it.

But the best thing Grandmother ever made for me was my crayon apron. It had a pinafore top, ties at the neck, a sash at the waist, and an inset along the bottom of the apron with 48 slots for individual crayons. I was the most popular kid in class when I wore my crayon apron to school.

All the girls wanted to try my apron on and use the crayons, and I proudly let them while bragging about Grandmother. Even the boys wanted to borrow some of my crayons, since I had so many colors.

Grandmother also crocheted beautiful afghans, bedspreads and darling angels. After I grew up, I mailed Grandmother pictures and patterns of crocheted items from women's magazines. I called her often, but she never mentioned those magazine clippings.

Many years later, Grandmother passed away. As I helped my Aunt Gerry set the supper table the night before services, she took out some lovely crocheted place mats.

"Where did you get these pretty things?" I asked her.

"Well, you ought to know," she said. "You sent Mama the pattern years ago. But she never used the directions, she just looked at the pictures and figured it out."

Grandmother, even in death, was reaching out to me again with her talent for making beautiful crocheted items from the pictures I had sent her. I miss her still, and I cherish and use every afghan she ever made me. And her crocheted angels have a place of honor on my Christmas tree every year.

Beverly's daughter, Emily, and grandmother show off
a crocheted masterpiece in 1989.

OLE BABE'S SLEIGH BELLS

Rudolph the Red-Nosed Reindeer would be proud of this trusted horse and her wintry trek.

LARRY BOONE PAULS VALLEY, OKLAHOMA

About 50 years ago my grandpa had a farm workhorse named Babe. At the holidays, Ole Babe would let all of the cousins and grandkids ride her around for fun. One day, Grandpa got a tractor. It wasn't long before Ole Babe spent more time in the barn and less time in the fields.

Summer and fall came and went. For weeks Grandpa prepared the farm for cold weather, and soon Christmas was just around the corner. We celebrated our holidays at the farm, so my grandparents planned to go into town for supplies.

Snow fell early that morning, and by afternoon everything was covered in a pure white blanket. Grandpa wanted to take the truck parked next to Babe's manger into town, but it wouldn't start.

He uncovered that dusty old sleigh they had used years ago when Babe was young, asking, "Well, girl, do you think you can still give it a pull?" Before long, the sleigh was clean and Ole Babe was ready to go.

My grandparents and their dog, Rusty, climbed into the sleigh and headed to town. Babe pulled them across the creek and through the woods for about an hour until they reached the little country store.

They bought food and holiday supplies, then loaded the sleigh, covered themselves with one of Grandma's handmade quilts, and headed back to the farm.

Ole Babe pulled hard on the sleigh, the wind blowing into her face. Soon the night was so dark and the snow was falling so hard that they couldn't see where they were going, but they heard the sleigh bells on Ole Babe's harness. The journey seemed to last forever, but finally a light appeared. My grandparents sighed in relief that Ole Babe knew the way home.

As Grandpa removed the harness from Babe's neck, the look of a young horse shone in her eyes. He gave her a bucket of fresh oats and thanked her for getting them back safely. He never forgot the sound of the sleigh bells that reassured him during the long, cold journey home.

For many years, Grandma retold the story of the ride and Ole Babe's sleigh bells, how they reminded them about Christmas as well as the importance of family and home.

So whenever you hear sleigh bells, remember that Christmas is around the corner and someone you can depend on is waiting in a manger!

Taste of the Country

LETTER-STAMPED BUTTER COOKIES

PREP 30 min. + chilling
BAKE 10 min./batch
MAKES about 2½ dozen

- 1 cup butter, softened
- 1 cup confectioners' sugar
- 1 large egg, room temperature
- 3 cups all-purpose flour
- ¼ tsp. salt
  Optional: Decorating icing and sprinkles

1. In a large bowl, cream butter and confectioners' sugar until light and fluffy, 5-7 minutes. Beat in egg. Combine flour and salt; gradually add to creamed mixture and mix well. Divide dough into thirds. Shape each into a ball, then flatten into a disk. Cover and refrigerate for 30 minutes.

2. Preheat oven to 350°. On a lightly floured surface, roll 1 portion of the dough to ¼-in. thickness. Cut with floured 2½-in. shaped cutters.

3. Place 1 in. apart on greased baking sheets. Press stamp into cookie. Repeat with remaining portions of dough. Bake until set, 8-10 minutes. Remove to wire racks to cool completely. Decorate as desired.

1 COOKIE 118 cal., 6g fat (4g sat. fat), 22mg chol., 71mg sod., 14g carb. (4g sugars, 0 fiber), 2g pro.

BRUSSELS SPROUTS AND TANGERINES

TAKES 30 min. **MAKES** 4 servings

- 1 lb. fresh Brussels sprouts, halved
- 1 cup shredded celery root
- ⅓ cup finely chopped onion
- 4 tsp. olive oil
- 1½ tsp. grated tangerine zest
- 2 tangerines, peeled and sectioned

1. In a large saucepan, bring ½ in. of water to a boil. Add the Brussels sprouts; cover and cook until crisp-tender, 8-10 minutes, then drain.

2. In a large nonstick skillet, saute the celery root and onion in oil until tender. Add tangerine zest and Brussels sprouts. Cover and cook until the vegetables are tender, 5-6 minutes. Gently stir in tangerines; serve immediately.

1 CUP 132 cal., 5g fat (1g sat. fat), 0 chol., 58mg sod., 21g carb. (9g sugars, 6g fiber), 5g pro. **DIABETIC EXCHANGES** 1 starch, 1 fat

HONEY-ORANGE GLAZED PORK LOIN

PREP 10 min. **BAKE** 1¼ hours
MAKES 12 servings

- 1 cup orange juice
- ½ cup cider vinegar
- ½ cup packed brown sugar
- ¼ cup honey
- 2 Tbsp. chili powder
- 1 Tbsp. ground coriander
- 1 Tbsp. ground cumin
- 1½ tsp. ground cinnamon
- 1 boneless pork loin roast (4 lbs.)
- 1 tsp. salt
- ¼ tsp. pepper

1. In a small saucepan, combine the first 8 ingredients. Bring to a boil. Reduce heat; simmer, uncovered, until the glaze is reduced to 1 cup, 45 minutes.

2. Meanwhile, preheat oven to 350°. Sprinkle the pork with salt and pepper. Place on rack in shallow roasting pan lined with heavy-duty foil. Roast until a thermometer reads 145°, 1¼-1¾ hours, brushing with the glaze 2-3 times after first hour of roasting. Let stand 10-15 minutes before slicing.

4 OZ. COOKED PORK 263 cal., 7g fat (3g sat. fat), 75mg chol., 258mg sod., 19g carb. (17g sugars, 1g fiber), 30g pro. **DIABETIC EXCHANGES** 4 lean meat, 1 starch

CORNBREAD CHICKEN BAKE

PREP 20 min. **BAKE** 45 min.
MAKES 10 servings

1¼	lbs. boneless skinless chicken breasts
6	cups cubed cornbread
8	bread slices, cubed
1	medium onion, chopped
2	cans (10¾ oz. each) condensed cream of chicken soup, undiluted
1	cup chicken broth
2	Tbsp. butter, melted
1½	to 2 tsp. rubbed sage
1	tsp. salt
½	to 1 tsp. pepper

1. Preheat oven to 350°. Place chicken in a skillet; cover with water. Bring to a boil. Reduce heat and cover. Simmer until a thermometer reads 165°, 12-14 minutes. Drain, then cut chicken into cubes.
2. In a large bowl, combine the remaining ingredients. Add chicken. Transfer to greased 13x9-in. baking dish.
3. Bake, uncovered, until heated through, 45 minutes.

1 CUP 392 cal., 9g fat (3g sat. fat), 40mg chol., 1307mg sod., 57g carb. (3g sugars, 4g fiber), 20g pro.

PEAR-STUFFED FRENCH TOAST WITH BRIE, BERRIES & PECANS

PREP 35 min. + chilling
BAKE 35 min. + standing
MAKES 10 servings

2	Tbsp. butter
4	medium pears, peeled and thinly sliced
3	Tbsp. brown sugar, divided
1	pkg. (8 oz.) cream cheese, softened
½	cup dried cranberries
⅓	cup chopped pecans, toasted
20	slices French bread (½ in. thick)
1	round (8 oz.) Brie cheese, rind removed and thinly sliced
3	large eggs
2	cups 2% milk
3	tsp. vanilla extract
½	tsp. ground cinnamon
¼	tsp. salt
	Maple syrup, optional

1. In a large skillet, heat butter over medium heat. Add pears and 2 Tbsp. brown sugar; cook and stir until pears are tender, 4-6 minutes. In a bowl, mix cream cheese, cranberries and pecans.
2. Place half the bread slices in a greased 13x9-in. baking dish. Layer with cream cheese mixture, pear mixture and Brie. Top with remaining bread slices. Whisk together the next 5 ingredients and remaining brown sugar. Pour over bread. Refrigerate, covered, overnight.
3. Preheat oven to 375°. Remove from the refrigerator while oven heats. Bake, uncovered, until top is golden brown, 35-40 minutes. Let stand 10 minutes before serving. If desired, serve with maple syrup.

1 SERVING 393 cal., 22g fat (11g sat. fat), 111mg chol., 476mg sod., 38g carb. (20g sugars, 4g fiber), 12g pro.

HOMEMADE EGGNOG

PREP 15 min. **COOK** 30 min. + chilling
MAKES 12 servings

- 12 **large eggs**
- 1½ **cups sugar**
- ½ **tsp. salt**
- 8 **cups whole milk, divided**
- 2 **Tbsp. vanilla extract**
- 1 **tsp. ground nutmeg**
- 2 **cups heavy whipping cream**
  Additional nutmeg, optional

1. In a heavy saucepan, whisk together eggs, sugar and salt. Gradually add 4 cups milk; cook and stir over low heat until a thermometer reads 160°-170°, 30-35 minutes. Do not allow to boil. Immediately transfer mixture to a large bowl.

2. Stir in vanilla, nutmeg and remaining milk. Place bowl in an ice-water bath, stirring until the milk mixture is cool. (If mixture separates, process in a blender until smooth.) Refrigerate, covered, until cold, at least 3 hours.

3. To serve, beat cream until soft peaks form. Whisk gently into the cooled milk mixture. If desired, sprinkle with additional nutmeg before serving.

1 CUP 411 cal., 25g fat (14g sat. fat), 247mg chol., 251mg sod., 35g carb. (35g sugars, 0 fiber), 13g pro.

STACKED CHRISTMAS TREE COOKIES

PREP 30 min. **BAKE** 10 min. + cooling
MAKES 9 servings

- 1 tube (16½ oz.) refrigerated sugar cookie dough
- ½ tsp. vanilla extract
- ½ cup all-purpose flour
   Green colored sugar
- 1 can (16 oz.) vanilla frosting
- 9 unwrapped Rolo candies
   Necco wafer candies
   Smarties candies
   Yellow food coloring
   Red nonpareils

1. Preheat oven to 350°. Place the dough in bowl; let stand to soften, 5-10 minutes. Beat in vanilla. Add flour; beat until blended.

2. On a floured surface, roll the dough to ¼-in. thickness. Using a floured 2-in. round cookie cutter, cut out 18 cookies. Repeat with 1½-in. and 1-in. round cookie cutters. For remaining dough, use a floured ½-in. star-shaped cookie cutter to cut out 9 stars.

3. Sprinkle round cookies with green sugar. Place 1 in. apart on ungreased baking sheets. Bake until the edges are light brown, 6-9 minutes. Remove to wire racks to cool completely.

4. For each tree, pipe frosting on top of a Rolo candy for trunk; top with a 2-in. cookie. Pipe frosting on top and bottom of a wafer; place in center of cookie. Top with another 2-in. cookie. Repeat with two 1½-in. cookies and two 1-in. cookies, using Smarties between layers.

5. For the stars, color a small amount of frosting yellow and pipe onto cookies; attach to top of trees using frosting. Thin extra frosting with water; drizzle over edges. Decorate with nonpareils.

1 CHRISTMAS TREE 466 cal., 18g fat (6g sat. fat), 6mg chol., 278mg sod., 72g carb. (48g sugars, 1g fiber), 3g pro.

WINTER SQUASH WITH MAPLE GLAZE

PREP 20 min. **BAKE** 50 min.
MAKES 6 servings

- 2 cups chopped peeled parsnips
- 2 cups cubed peeled kabocha squash
- 2 cups cubed peeled butternut squash
- ⅓ cup butter, cubed
- ½ cup maple syrup
- 1 Tbsp. minced fresh rosemary or 1 tsp. dried rosemary, crushed
- 1 garlic clove, minced
- ½ tsp. salt
- ¼ tsp. pepper
- ¾ cup coarsely chopped almonds

1. Preheat oven to 375°. In a bowl, combine parsnips and squashes. In a small saucepan, melt butter over medium heat; whisk in next 5 ingredients. Pour over vegetables and toss to coat.

2. Transfer to a greased 11x7-in. baking dish. Bake, covered, 40 minutes. Uncover; sprinkle with chopped almonds. Bake until vegetables are tender, 10-15 minutes longer.

¾ CUP 339 cal., 19g fat (7g sat. fat), 27mg chol., 290mg sod., 43g carb. (22g sugars, 7g fiber), 5g pro.

MINTY SNOWMEN

PREP 50 min. **MAKES** 9 snowmen

- 1 Tbsp. butter, softened
- 1 Tbsp. light corn syrup
- ½ tsp. mint extract
- ⅛ tsp. salt
- 1 cup confectioners' sugar
- Red, green, blue and/or purple liquid or gel food coloring
- Colored sprinkles, nonpareils and cake decorator candies

1. In a small bowl, combine the butter, corn syrup, extract and salt. Gradually stir in confectioners' sugar. Knead by hand until the mixture becomes pliable, 1-2 minutes.

2. For each color of dough, combine 1 Tbsp. of dough and the food coloring; knead until blended. Leave remaining dough white. Roll white dough into a log; remove a fourth of the log and set aside.

3. For the snowmen's bodies, divide the remaining log into 9 pieces and roll into balls. For the snowmen's heads, divide the reserved dough into 9 pieces and roll into balls. Stack 1 smaller ball on top of each larger ball.

4. Use the colored dough to form hats, scarves and earmuffs as desired. Use candies to make eyes, noses and buttons.

1 SNOWMAN 80 cal., 1g fat (1g sat. fat), 4mg chol., 55mg sod., 17g carb. (15g sugars, 0 fiber), 0 pro.

Handcrafted

CREATE A FEELING OF HOME

DECK THE TREE

WHAT YOU'LL NEED
2 yd. plaid fabric
Coordinating thread
Coordinating yarn
92 pingpong balls
Sewing machine

DIRECTIONS
1. Cut 3 strips of fabric 2 yd. long and 5⅞ in. wide. Place 2 strips right sides together and sew 1 short end together with a ¼-in. seam. Repeat with third piece to create a 6-yd.-long strip.
2. Fold strip lengthwise on itself with right sides together and sew a ¼-in. seam along the cut edge, leaving ends open to create a long tube. Turn right side out.
3. Cut short pieces of yarn and tie 1 piece at the end of the tube. Fill tube with pingpong balls and tie yarn tightly between each ball. Tie off end with yarn.

SOFTHEARTED HELLO

WHAT YOU'LL NEED

Yarn (1-2 skeins of each of 3 colors)
Heart-shaped foam wreath form
Card stock
Pink acrylic paint
Pompom maker
Hot glue gun
Paintbrush

DIRECTIONS

1. Make approximately 70 pompoms using instructions with pompom maker, keeping most 3½ cm in diameter, some 5½ cm, and a few 7 cm.

2. Hot-glue pompoms to wreath form. Glue smallest pompoms along inner edge to keep heart shape in the middle.

3. To make envelope detail, cut a cardstock rectangle 2x2¾ in. Draw flaps with a marker. Draw a heart in center; paint with 2 coats of acrylic paint, drying thoroughly between coats.

4. Hot-glue envelope to wreath.

HIDDEN TREASURES

WHAT YOU'LL NEED

24-muffin tin
Scrapbook paper in
    2 complementary colors
Double-sided tape
Glitter glue
Christmas stickers
Adhesive numbers
Craft glue
24 small magnets
24 buttons
Decorative ribbon
Candy
Small toys
Drill
Circle punch in 2 sizes

DIRECTIONS

1. Drill two holes at top of tin.

2. With larger circle punch, cut 24 circles of 1 scrapbook paper big enough to cover the tin's cups. Cut 24 smaller circles in a complementary paper. Secure each small circle on top of a larger circle with double-sided tape. Add glitter glue around edges of smaller circles; dry.

3. Embellish with stickers. Center numbers 1-24 on smaller circles; secure with craft glue. Adhere a magnet to each button; dry.

4. Thread ribbon through holes; tie in place. Place candy or toy in each cup. Use a button magnet to hold circles over each opening. Use ribbon to hang. Remove circles to reveal one cup each day as you count down to Christmas.

"*Life isn't a matter of milestones, but of moments.*"

—ROSE FITZGERALD KENNEDY

The land glows orange-gold as the sun rises over North Dakota's badlands.

GREG LATZA